nitty gritty books

15/10
50p

Brunch
My Cookbook
Family Favorites
Cookies
Cooking for 1 or 2
Chicken Cookery
Skillet Cookbook
Convection Oven
Household Hints
Seafood Cookbook
Quick Breads
Pasta & Rice
Pies & Cakes
Yogurt

Cocktails & Hors d'Oeuvres
Casseroles & Salads
Pressure Cooking
Food Processor Cookbook
Soups & Stews
Crepes & Omelets
Microwave Cooking
Vegetable Cookbook
Kid's Arts and Crafts
Bread Baking
The Crockery Pot Cookbook
Classic Greek Cooking
Low Carbohydrate Cookbook
Kid's Cookbook
Cheese Guide & Cookbook

Miller's German
Quiche & Souffle
To My Daughter With Love
Natural Foods
Chinese Vegetarian
Working Couples
Mexican
Fisherman's Wharf Cookbook
Barbecue Cookbook
Ice Cream Cookbook
Blender Cookbook
The Wok, a Chinese Cookbook
Japanese Country
Fondue Cookbook

designed with giving in mind

Nitty Gritty Productions ● P.O. Box 5457 ● Concord, California 94524

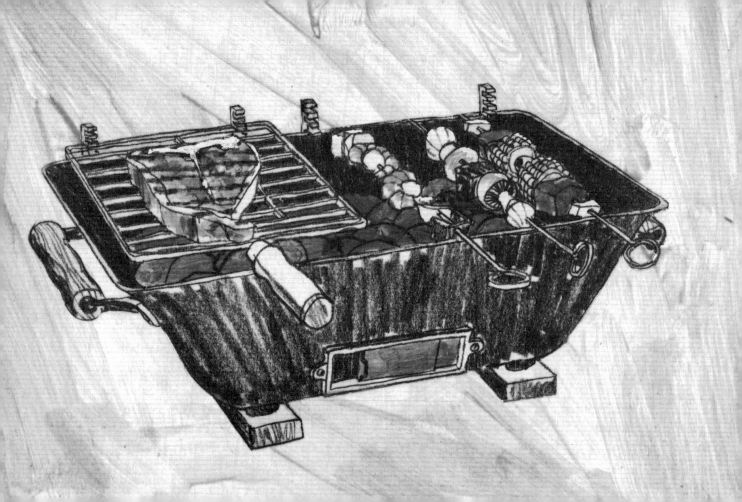

BARBECUE COOKBOOK

By Ed Callahan

Illustrated by Mike Nelson

I would like to thank the following people for their help and moral support during the preparation of the Barbecue Cookbook:

Hester Callahan
Leslie Callahan
Leslie Goss
Adrienne Laskier
Christine Poselenzny
Diane Garland
Ethel Ericson
Marsha Workman
Barbara Joy Voss
and
Bill and Diane Gasper

TABLE OF CONTENTS

INTRODUCTION 1
EQUIPMENT 4
BEEF 19
HAMBURGERS 40
HOT DOGS 49
LAMB 53
PORK 67
WILD GAME 76
SEAFOOD 83
POULTRY 103
VEGETABLES 123
SKEWER COOKING 132
APPETIZERS 146
DESSERT FRUITS 154
UNUSUAL CHARCOAL IMPLEMENTS 159
INDEX 177

INTRODUCTION TO BARBECUE COOKBOOK

At the beach, in the park, or in your own back yard, everyone enjoys a barbecue. The mere mention of the word is enough to evoke images of The Fourth of July, lazy summer afternoons and relaxed dinners with family and friends.

The smokey flavor that foods obtain when they have been cooked on a barbecue, are what make them so delicious. The intensity of this flavor may vary, according to the type of barbecue equipment you use. Almost without exception, barbecue equipment needs charcoal—and this is what produces the lovely smokey flavor.

Charcoal is probably man's oldest maufactured cooking and heating fuel. In its original form, it retained the size and shape of the wood materials from which it was made. The characteristics that made it popular to primitive peoples are still its major features today—slow, even burning, and ease of handling.

Today, charcoal is manufactured from bones, seeds, pulp mill wastes, nutshells, kelp, distillery wastes, cereals, and corncobs. It is widely used in industry for purfying and decoloring.

Thanks for the first charcoal briquet goes to the father of the mass produced automobile, Henry Ford. Being a frugal man, Ford made use of the scrap wood left over from the production of automobile frames. He had it converted to charcoal, ground into powder, mixed with a binder and pressed into the now familiar shape of briquets. He also manufactured thin steel collapsible stoves with *Ford* stamped on the cover. An indispensible item for family campouts in the 20's and 30's.

Today, cooking with charcoal, whether done on a simple wire grill in the woods, or on an elaborate backyard barbecue is one of America's favorite ways to cook. In addition to being good eating, barbecue cooking is fun. Food prepared and eaten in the out-of-doors is somehow better.

Ed Callahan

2

EQUIPMENT

The basic ingredient to a good meal is comradeship. These various cooking implements permit convival cooking and seem to bring all the participants closer to one another. The cook, by preparing the food ahead of time, may also join in the fun. The warm glow of the barbecue, plus an excellent dinner, can make a memorable occasion out of an otherwise ordinary evening.

Barbecue equipment is of two types: grills, both open and covered in which food is cooked directly over or near the coals, and heat source implements such as the Mongolian Hot Pot or Wok in which food is cooked by placing the implement over a charcoal fire.

BRAZIERS

The least expensive and simplest unit is the brazier. It is usually round, has short legs and is made of painted steel. It has a bowl 3" to 6" in depth and it is designed to stand on a table. It comes with a round wire grill which fits on an adjustable center post.

SEMI-COVERED BRAZIERS

These units are larger than the simple round brazier. They usually have full height legs with or without wheels, and a hood that covers about half of the circumference. The hood usually has provision for a large single skewer and rotisserie motor. They are not as useful as the covered units described next, however they are acceptable in situations where only grilling is done, or use is limited to a few cookouts each year.

BRAZIER OVEN COMBINATIONS

The most useful outdoor barbecuing implements are the combination brazier-ovens. They vary from simple covered braziers to elaborate jumbo covered braziers with spits, motorized skewers and built in thermometers. Some are large enough to cook 15 steaks or 5 chickens at one time.

As the price goes up, more features appear. The heavier the steel, aluminum or earthenware, the better the heat retention. Provision for more accurate heat control is obtained by means of adjustable vents. The coals rest on a steel or cast iron grid unit, so that the ashes fall through, leaving a clean area for the coals at all times.

As is the case with most purchases, buy the best unit that you can afford. In the long run, it well save you money.

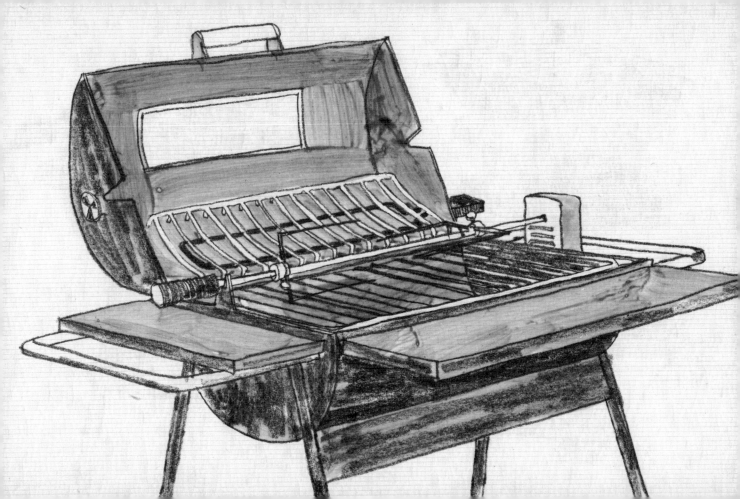

HIBACHI

The hibachi is a dual purpose barbecuing implement. It can be used in exactly the same way as a brazier for grilling small cuts of meat, vegetables, or fruit, or it can be used as the heat source for ordinary pots and unusual cooking utensils such as the Mongolian Hot Pot or Genghis Kahn.

Hibachis are excellent for preparing appetizers and other small items, many people find their small size to be of advantage for use in apartments and on picnics for general barbecuing.

Although hibachis sold in America are generally square in shape and made of cast iron or cast aluminum, the Japanese use round clay hibachis. If you would like to purchase an authentic clay unit, you will probably find it at a Japanese store or trade center.

For your next cocktail party, fill a platter full of chunks of sausage, meat balls, or other small meat cuts, next to a glowing hibachi. You guests will cook their own appetizers and enjoy every bite.

For steaks and chops, try a double hibachi. These larger units are adequate for bachelors, bachelorettes, and couples.

GAS AND ELECTRIC EQUIPMENT

Gas and electric outdoor equipment is becoming increasingly popular. The almost instant heat source is located either above or below self-cleaning lava rack coals. A heat control on both types of equipment allows a high position for searing and cleaning and a low position for broiling, roasting and baking. A cooking flavor similar to that of charcoal is produced without the associated residue and ash. Most of the equipment available is of the Braizer oven combination variety and is at the high end of the price range.

Electric equipment uses 110 volt household current and gas models are available in either natural gas or refillable LP gas canisters. Both types of gas equipment are available in either stationary or movable models. Electric, because of its versatility, is normally found only in the movable model.

THE KOMADO OVEN

The Komado Oven is a large earthenware pot with a heavy lid. As the grill-to-fire height is not adjustable, it is not recommended for grilling. It is an oven which bakes food while smoking it. You can increase the smoke flavor by adding wet aromatic wood chips.

Temperature in the oven is controlled by regulating the draft openings in the base and lid.

If some coals remain after cooking, you can preserve them for your next cookout by closing the vents and the lid.

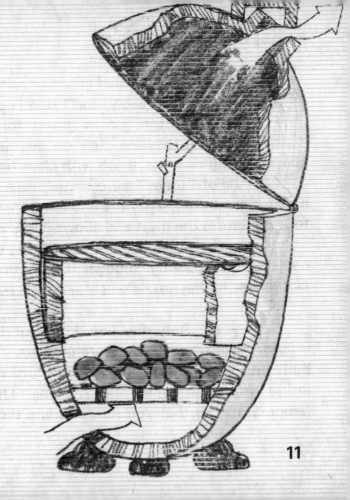

11

BARBECUE ACCESORIES

A good pair of insulated gloves or mitts: Asbestos padding is good but not necessary. The cheapest kind probably won't stand up to continued washing.

A pair of cotton garden gloves for placing non-lighted briquets in your unit. It doesn't matter if they get dirty on the outside. Just leave them in your charcoal bag or holder. You'll do a better job with clean hands.

A pair of "tongs" are essential, especially for hot briquet handling. The longer the handles, the better. They are also good for turning chops, steaks, chicken, etc. A barbecue fork punctures the meat and allows juices to drop on the coals, causing flare-ups.

A squirt gun is good for dampening coals that become too hot or flare-up. It has a habit of disappearing, though. (Check your kids' pockets.) A soft-drink bottle with a clothes-sprinkling nozzle will also do the job.

There are basically two kinds of barbecue thermometers: air temperature and interior meat temperature thermometers. The air temperature types are quite often found built into the hood of the covered units. Also, they may be purchased separately to put inside your unit when spit roasting. This will then tell you the approximate oven temperature, so that you may regulate the coals or vents in your unit for an even heat.

Knowing the heat level allows you to figure the time necessary for cooking to the desired doneness.

The best barbecue thermometer is the insertion-type interior thermometer. These you insert near the end of cooking to determine doneness (rare, medium) of thick meats, such as flat roasts, turkey, whole chickens, etc. They can be used on rotisserie roasts or spit-roasted birds, but they are clumsy and may become damaged if the dial gets too close to the coals or strikes the side of the barbecue while turning.

A long handled basting brush. A good long-handled brush is useful on hot fires. Wash well directly after using. Dishwashers won't hurt them.

Several wooden spoons. In some ways wooden spoons can be just as important as a sharp knife. They won't scratch your pots (even teflon, if you're careful). They're strong, clean easily and, most important, they have a primitive, comforting aura about them which helps to make life more enjoyable.

A roll of aluminum wire. Essential for tying up stubborn birds and roasts. String may do the job, but wire is better. It's rather difficult to retie a hot, dripping 6-lb. roast! But be careful. The wire is strong enough to tear the meat if overtightened.

Some regular pliers with a wire cutting notch. Great for tightening up loose bolts on your various apparatus and for tying the wire around your roasts or birds.

Some small-mesh flexible wire cloth. Just the thing for those odd size fish or scallops or toasted sandwiches. It can also be used to form a frame for foil "tents", to serve as a fire basket, etc.

A good fish rack: These are open metal racks in the shape of a fish with legs on both top and bottom. They stand right in the coals and you just turn them over. They are hinged for opening and have a clip to hold them closed. They will accept almost any type of medium-sized, whole fish.

Two hinged metal broiling racks, one large and one small: They should have fairly long wooden handles and a close mesh. Ideal for burgers, hot dogs, fish fillets, and vegetables.

A good quality chicken basket for your rotisserie: These baskets are hinged for opening and allow cooking of odd-sized chicken parts.

A small pot with long handle in which to keep your baste warm. There is usually a place on the grill or in the coals for this pot. It's a good container for your brush too. Keeping the baste warm and stirred guarantees the best results. I use a very small heavy cast iron pot for my barbecue sauce. Once heated it can be removed from the coals and still stay warm. They are available at industrial hardware stores. Ask for a plumber's hot lead pot. Get the smallest size.

WOOD CHIPS

It's always a good idea to have some presoaked hardwood chips to add to your fire. Hickory is the most commonly available, either as dry wood chips in a bag or as a moist sawdust-like material sold in sealed plastic containers. Actually, as mentioned in the SMOKE COOKING section, any aromatic hardwood (such as apple, cherry, plum, etc.) can be used. Soft woods such as pine are usually resinous and will impart disagreeable tastes to the food. (For this reason, these soft woods are not advisable for cookouts at the beach.)

PREPARING THE NEW BARBECUE

To protect the bottom of your new barbecue, it is advisable to place a layer of sand or small pebbles in it before using it. Drippings from the meat will be burned up by the fire, and the fine charcoal dust will settle into your layer of pebbles or sand. Once or twice a season, you should empty the pan and replace the pebbles or sand.

The grill is practically self-cleaning. Just set it over the coals for about five minutes before you are ready to cook on it and the old residue and drippings will burn off. Then rub it quickly with steel wool and you are ready to go.

GRILLING

Grilling is the way most people cook out-of-doors. You can grill on a wire rack placed on rocks over the coals, or you can use an open charcoal brazier. Grilling is best for steaks, chops, hamburgers and hot dogs. Use plenty of charcoal and sear the meat close to the coals on each side. Then raise the grill and cook until done.

SMOKE COOKING

The Chinese use an igloo-type oven big enough for a man to enter. Meat is hung from hooks in a large chamber and smoke from an outside fire is drawn through the chamber. This slow method of smoking with very little heat is the secret behind Chinese pork and duck delicacies.

The principal of smoke cooking is simply cooking with a cover over the food. Damp hickory chips or small green twigs from wild cherry, hickory, or sugar maple trees can be used for that wonderful pungent flavor. For a light smoke flavor, add them just before the food is done. For a deeper smoke flavor, chips may be added just before the cooking is started.

You can smoke cook on a simple, open brazier by using a tent of foil or you can use a modern covered barbecue.

Any large rectangular or oval covered brazier can be used to great advantage in smoke cooking by moving the hot coals to one side of the unit, placing the food on the other side of the unit and closing the lid. This way, the food is never burned. It bakes slowly and is barbecued through and through. This works particularly well for chicken and other poultry as well as for roasts. Steaks, chops, or hamburgers are first grilled directly over the coals and then moved to one side, closing the lid, and baking until done.

BEEF

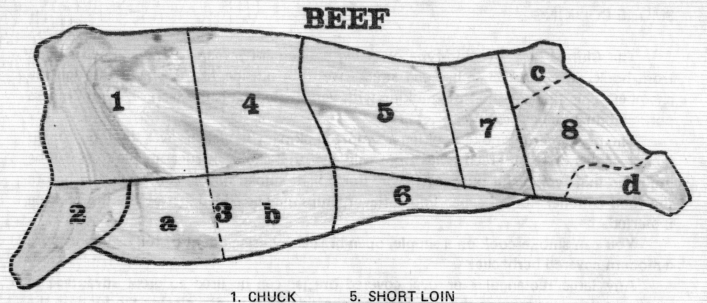

1. CHUCK
2. SHANK
3. PLATE
   a. brisket
   b. navel end
4. RIB

5. SHORT LOIN
6. FLANK
7. LOIN END
8. ROUND
   c. rump
   d. hind shank

BEEF

Beef is the all time favorite meat for Americans and barbecuing is no exception. Tasty, juicy beef steaks and roasts are a part of the majority of cookout menus.

In selecting beef, it is helpful to know the various grades. Many stores feature U.S.D.A. graded beef. Once you understand the grading technique used, you'll have no trouble selecting the proper grade. Nutritionally, all grades are similar. The difference is in tenderness and flavor.

U.S.D.A. Prime is the most expensive grade. This is the beef that comes from those beautiful prize winning cattle at state fairs. It is well marbled with fat, and when properly prepared, can be cut with a fork. Most butchers do not carry this grade, as it is in short supply.

U.S.D.A. Choice is the next quality, and when it is properly aged, the better cuts are excellent. For steaks and roasts, you'll probably find this grade to be tender, tasty, and suitable for the grandest occasion. Choice beef is well marbled with fat, but not quite as heavily marbled as prime. It is the grade which is carried in most butcher shops and supermarkets in the United States.

U.S.D.A. Good has almost no fat running through it. It looks lean. To the uninitiated it would appear to be the best of the three grades; however, the lack of fat makes for tougher meat. Use U.S.D.A. Good for pot roasts, swiss steak and stew. If you have to grill it or roast it, first treat it with meat tenderizer, or marinade.

There are other U.S.D.A. grades, of lower quality, and although they are just as nutritious as the better grades, they require long and careful cooking, and have no place on the barbecue.

UNGRADED BEEF

If your butcher does not sell graded meat, the key to selection of high quality beef is the fat marbling. If the beef has heavy veins of fat running through it, it's probably good for barbecuing. If you buy a side of beef at a time, you probably know that the better the grade you buy, the less meat you get because the fat content is higher in the better grades, and there is more waste.

SELECTION OF CUTS

For broiling, make your selection from the tenderloin (Filet Mignon), T Bone,

Porterhouse, Sirloin and Club steaks. With tenderizer or marinade, the flank steak can be added to the list. Do not pick a steak from the self service counter. Instead, ask for your steaks to be cut at least 1" thick (never less) and preferably 1 1/2" thick. It is difficult to properly grill a thin steak. You won't go wrong at 2", however when steaks are really thick, you'll want to slice them after grilling and serve one large one to several people.

BARBECUING STEAK

Use plenty of charcoal. There should be no spaces between the briquets and the coals should cover a larger area than the area that the steak occupies on the grill. The steak should be at room temperature. First slash through the fat on the outside of the steak at 1" intervals to keep the steak from curling. Place the steak on the grill and lower the grill to within about 3 inches of the fire. If your coals are hot enough, the steak will char very rapidly. This seals in the juices. The fat from the meat will drip on the coals and they will blaze up. At this stage, let them blaze away. In a minute or two, the meat will be a rich brown-black charred color. Now, turn it over (with a pair of tongs - not a fork) and sear the other side. If you like rare (blood red center) steak, you are through. If you like medium (pink and juicy center) or well done (cooked completely in the center), do the following:

(1) If you have a covered grill, move the steak completely off the coals to the furthermost point on the grill away from the fire. Open your vents, and close the lid. The blazing fire should go out immediately. If it doesn't, close the vents for a few seconds and then open them. Leave the steak inside for about 10 minutes for a 1 1/2" steak for medium and longer for well done. Don't be afraid to cut the steak open with a knife to see how its coming. Now, remove it to a serving platter and add salt and pepper, or brush it with a small amount of melted butter in which you've previously mixed garlic salt, salt, and pepper.

(2) If you have a brazier, raise the grill and rotate the steaks away from the coals by turning the grill. Now let the fire go out. Use a squirt gun if necessary. Then rotate the steak back over the coals and cook in the raised position for about 5 minutes on each side for medium for a 1 1/2" steak. Follow directions for testing and seasoning in (1) above.

A properly grilled steak, over charcoal, is one of life's great experiences. You'll probably make a few mistakes, but once you get the timing down, you'll produce consistent results.

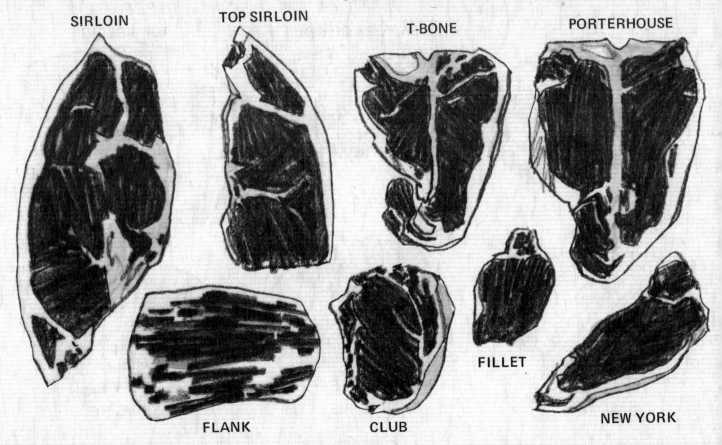

STEAKS

SIRLOIN · TOP SIRLOIN · T-BONE · PORTERHOUSE · FLANK · CLUB · FILLET · NEW YORK

ROASTS

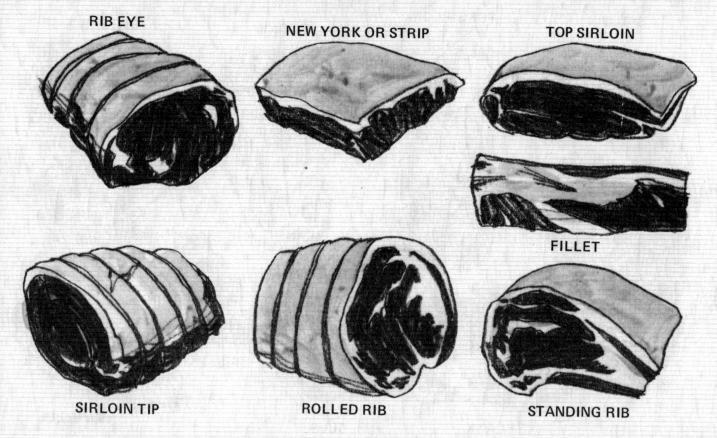

RIB EYE

NEW YORK OR STRIP

TOP SIRLOIN

FILLET

SIRLOIN TIP

ROLLED RIB

STANDING RIB

BARBECUED ROASTS

Meats are best roasted at low temperatures. Select a standing rib, rolled rib, or sirloin tip roast of at least 5 pounds. It is possible to barbecue roasts on a rotisserie on a hooded brazier, however, a layer of fat must be provided around the roast to keep it from drying out. Just tell your butcher that you are spit roasting, and he'll prepare the roast for you. The best way to barbecue roasts is in a covered grill or barbecue oven. A spit is not necessary, although it certainly won't hinder the process.

If you are using a rotisserie on a hooded brazier, place a large pile of hot coals at the rear of the brazier, and place a long foil pan (make it yourself from heavy duty foil) under the meat. Cook the roast until your insertion type meat thermometer tells you it is done. It should take from 25 to 30 minutes per pound for medium, or you are cooking it too fast.

If you are using a covered grill or barbecue oven, place all of the coals at one end and put the roast on the grill at the other. Close your vents slightly so that the fire will burn slowly. Again, use the meat thermometer to tell you when it is done.

Always let a roast sit for 10 minutes before slicing it to allow the juices to set.

There you have the basic methods for cooking steaks and roasts over the coals. Now let's look at some refinements.

WINE AND PEPPER STEAK

2 1/2-3 lbs. boneless sirloin steak, 1 1/2-2 inches thick
2 T. coarsely ground pepper
1 tsp. salt
1/4 cup melted butter
1/4 cup olive oil
2 T. broth or water
1/3 cup white wine
1/4 cup brandy

Rub pepper into both sides of the steak and sprinkle with salt. Sear both sides of steak over hot coals. Brush both sides with mixture of melted butter and oil. Raise the grill and cook for about 5 minutes on each side. Place on a warm platter when done. Combine remaining butter and oil with broth, wine, and brandy. Pour over steak and ignite. Serves 4-6.

ROQUEFORT FLANK STEAK

1 flank steak, about 2 lbs.
oil and vinegar salad dressing
1/4 cup butter
1/2 cup Roquefort cheese
1 garlic clove, minced
1 T. chopped chives
1 T. brandy

Marinate steak in your favorite oil and vinegar dressing for 6 hours. Cream butter and cheese until completely blended. Mix in garlic, chives, and brandy. Barbecue steak over very hot coals, 5 minutes on each side. Place on heated platter and slice against the grain in diagonal strips. Spoon Roquefort butter over steak and let it melt a little before serving. Serves 4.

BEEF SHANKS AND SUMMER SQUASH

4 medium crookneck or zucchini squash, cut in half lengthwise
salt
prepared mustard
1/2 to 3/4 cup fine dry bread crumbs
1/2 tsp. horseradish
1/2 tsp. basil
6 T. butter or margarine
1 tsp. salt
8 to 10 whole black peppercorns
1 bay leaf
1 carrot, sliced
2 cups water
1/2 medium onion, sliced
4 slices of meaty beef shank, each 1-inch thick

Cook beef shanks in a wide shallow pan, adding water, onion, carrot, bay leaf, whole black peppers, and salt. Boil, cover and simmer slowly about 1 1/2 hours until tender. Cool slightly in liquid and then remove shanks and remove the bone. Melt butter or margarine and blend in mustard, horseradish, basil. Dip shanks into butter, coat with fine dry bread crumbs. Dip squash in the same mixture and sprinkle with salt. Place beef and vegetables, cut side down, on barbecue about 6 inches above the coals (they should be medium-hot temperature). Turn as needed, meat will be browned and the squash will be tender and browned, about 10 to 15 minutes. Butter squash and pour excess butter over meat and vegetables and serve. Serves 4.

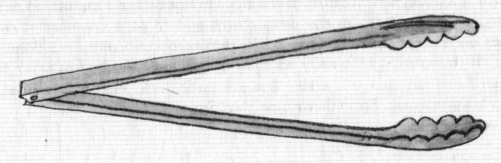

PEPPER STEAK WITH CREAM

2 1/2-3 lbs. fillet or top sirloin steak
2 tsp. salt
1/4 cup peppercorns, cracked
3 T. oil
1/4 cup brandy
1 cup cream
minced parsley

Remove the fat and bone from the steak, sprinkle with salt. Press the pepper into both sides of the steak. Brown on top of the stove in hot oil for 1 minute on each side. No longer. This is simply to secure the peppercorns and to get some meat juices for your sauce. Place on the grill over medium coals, turning occasionally until done. Test with knife after 10 minutes. Add brandy to the hot oil and drippings in your frying pan. Ignite. When flame has died, add cream and stir until thick. Place steak on a platter and pour the cream sauce over. Sprinkle with parsley. Serves 4.

BARBECUED ROAST IN FOIL

4-5 lb. rolled roast
1 tsp. pepper
1 tsp. salt
1/2 cup tomato sauce
1/4 cup soy sauce
1 T. prepared mustard
2 T. butter
1 clove garlic, crushed
2-3 T. chopped celery
3 carrots, sliced
2 onions, sliced

Saute onion, celery and carrots with garlic in butter for 7 minutes. Combine soy sauce, tomato sauce, mustard, salt and pepper and add to vegetables. Brown beef on all sides over the coals. Put part of vegetable sauce on a large piece of heavy-duty foil. Place meat in center of foil and cover with rest of sauce. Fold foil over meat, sealing edges so no juice can escape. Cook over low coals, turning occasionally for 1/2-2 1/2 hours. Serves 8.

31

GRILLED FILET MIGNON

4 medium sized filet mignons
2 T. melted butter
Marinade:
1/4 cup red wine
1/4 cup wine vinegar
4 bay leaves, crushed
1/2 tsp. salt
1/2 tsp. pepper

Marinate filets overnight in the refrigerator. One hour before barbecuing, remove from refrigerator and let stand at room temperature. Grill over hot coals 3-4 minutes on each side, basting as they cook. Filet mignon should be served rare to medium. Serves 4.

ANCHOVY BUTTERED CHUCK STEAK

1 chuck steak, 1-inch thick
unseasoned meat tenderizer
1/2 cup soft butter

1 tsp. lemon juice
1 can anchovies, minced
minced parsley

Prepare anchovy butter first. Combine butter, lemon juice, anchovies and parsley and blend well. Chill. Tenderize steak. Grill over hot coals until done to your taste. Spread with anchovy butter and cut into serving slices. Serves 2.

BARBECUED SIRLOIN WITH ROSEMARY

1 boneless top sirloin steak about 2 inches thick
2 T. fresh rosemary or 2 tsp. dried rosemary

salt
pepper

Rub rosemary into meat on both sides. Place meat over coals and cover with heavy aluminum foil and barbecue for 15 minutes on each side for medium meat. Put on carving board, sprinkle with pepper and salt. Slice diagonally.

STEAK AND CHEESE SANDWICHES

1 flank steak, about 1 1/2 lbs.
1/2 lb. Meunster cheese, sliced thin
powdered cumin
hot French bread

   Tenderize or marinate flank steak before cooking. Grill over hot coals, about 5 minutes on each side. Have bread and cheese ready. Cheese strips should be laid on French bread and sprinkled with cumin. Slice steak diagonally against the grain into thin strips. Place on top of cheese. Serves 4.

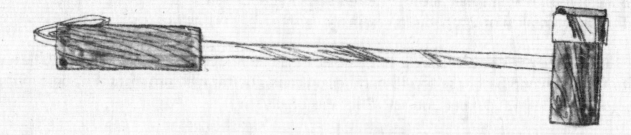

FLANK STEAK STUFFED WITH MUSHROOMS AND CHEESE

1 flank steak, 3 lbs.
1/2 lb. mushrooms, sliced
2 T. butter
2 T. blue cheese
1 clove crushed garlic
salt and pepper

Have your butcher make a pocket in your steak. Saute mushrooms in 1 T. butter, adding cheese, remaining butter and garlic. Season with salt and pepper. Fill the pocket with mixture and close with skewers. Sprinkle meat with salt and pepper and broil 3" from coals, until done. Slice in thin diagonal slices against the grain. Serves 4-6.

TERIYAKI MARINADE

1/2 tsp. powdered ginger
1/3 cup sherry
1/2 tsp. pepper
1 cup soy sauce
1/3 cup pineapple juice
2 T. brown sugar
1 onion, grated
1 garlic clove, minced

Combine all ingredients and pour over steak. Refrigerate several hours or overnight in a covered non-metal container. Remove meat from the refrigerator and let stand at room temperature at least 1 hour before barbecuing.

BEEF MARINADE WITH BEER (FOR ECONOMY CUTS)

1 clove garlic
1 can beer
1 tsp. salt
3 cloves garlic pressed

1/2 cup salad oil
1 T. sugar
2 T. lemon juice

Mix oil slowly into beer. Add remaining ingredients and stir. Marinate meat overnight. This is good for chuck roasts, or any U.S.D.A. Good steak, chop, or roast.

STEAK SAUCE

1/2 cup red wine
1/2 cup catsup
1/2 cup beer

1 tsp. garlic vinegar
dash of Tabasco sauce
2 T. butter

Bring all ingredients to a boil in a saucepan. Lower heat and simmer for 10 minutes. Pour over barbecued steak or roast.

GASPER'S BARBECUE SAUCE

1 garlic clove, minced
1 medium onion, chopped
2 T. butter
1/2 cup Worcestershire sauce
1/4 cup beer
1/4 cup vinegar
1 14-oz. bottle catsup

Tabasco to taste
1/2 tsp. barbecue spice
dash cayenne pepper
1/2 tsp. dry mustard
1/4 tsp. salt
2 T. brown sugar
1/2 tsp. liquid smoke

Saute garlic and onion (in butter) until limp. Add all remaining ingredients except liquid smoke. Bring to a boil, add liquid smoke and simmer for 15 minutes. Remove from heat and cool. Makes 3 cups. This sauce improves with age. Keep in the refrigerator.

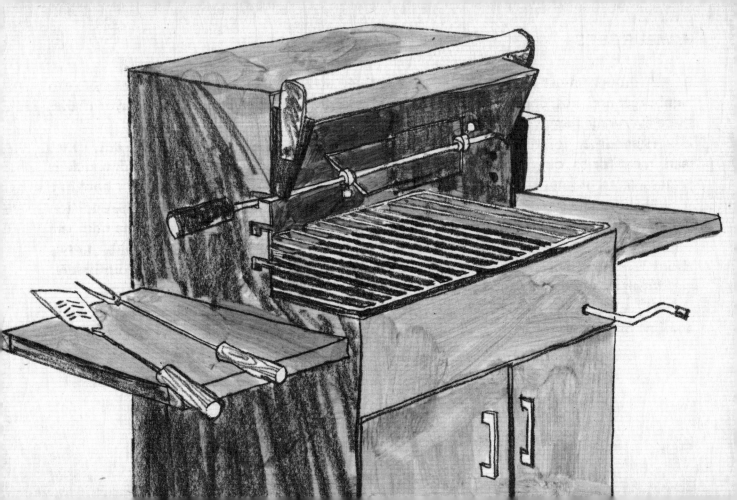

HAMBURGERS

Although most of us would prefer steak and roasts, we seem to end up with hamburger and hot dogs. The barbecue is a blessing because the charcoal flavor makes these everyday staples into delicious specialties.

Hamburger for the barbecue should contain some - but not too much - fat. Extra lean meat dries out quickly and must be basted. For this reason, ground chuck is preferable to ground round steak and is normally the correct choice for outdoor cooking.

Never make hamburgers smaller than ¼ lb. per person. They'll dry out. The addition of one egg and ¼ cup bread crumbs per pound of hamburger helps hold the hamburgers together, although undoctored patties usually survive on the grill. Make your ¼ lb. patties about ½" thick. Sear them as you would a steak and then raise the grill on your brazier and finish cooking. Normally 4 to 6 minutes on each side is sufficient cooking time.

Hamburgers should always be basted. Use your favorite barbecue sauce or a small amount of salad oil.

CHEDDAR BURGERS

1 egg
1 lb. ground chuck
1 tsp. salt
1/4 lb. cheddar cheese
1/2 tsp. pepper

Grate the cheese. Combine all ingredients and form into 4 patties. Double the recipe, if desired. Serve on hamburger buns.

MUSHROOM BURGERS

1 lb. ground chuck
1/4 tsp. salt
1 egg

1 cup fresh mushrooms, minced
1 T. butter

Saute mushrooms in butter for about 5 minutes. Let cool. Mix well with meat, salt, and egg. Form into four patties and grill until done. Serve on hamburger buns.

WINEBURGERS

2 lbs. ground chuck
1 cup bread crumbs
1 egg
1/4 cup dry red wine
2 T. chopped onion
1 tsp. salt
1/2 tsp. pepper
Sauce:
2 T. chopped onion
1/2 cup butter
1/4 cup wine

Mix together meat, bread crumbs, egg, wine, 2T. onion, salt and pepper. Shape into 8 patties. To make sauce, saute onion in butter until transparent. Add wine. Use sauce as a baste while you cook and serve as a sauce over cooked hamburgers. Serves 8.

PIZZA BURGERS

2 lbs. ground chuck
1/3 cup Parmesan cheese
1/4 cup chopped onion
1/2 cup green pepper, minced
1 tsp. salt
1 tsp. oregano
dash pepper
1 6-oz. can tomato paste
8 slices Mozarella cheese
8 tomato slices

Combine meat in a large bowl with Parmesan cheese, onion, green pepper, salt, pepper, oregano, and tomato paste. Shape into 8 patties. Broil over medium hot coals on one side. Turn over and top with tomato slices and cheese. Cook until cheese is melted. Serve on hamburger buns.

STUFFED HAMBURGERS

Although stuffings can be used in small 1/4 lb. hamburgers to be served in hamburger buns, they are best used with 1/3 lb. to 1/2 lb. portions and served as hamburger steaks. Your guests will never know they are eating hamburger.

Divide one pound of ground chuck into 4 sections (for 1/2 lb. steaks). Place each section between two sheets of waxed paper and pat into 4 rectangles each 1/4" thick. Place filling between two patties, seal edges all around, and you have two large hamburger steaks.

If you have trouble with meat crumbling on the grill, add one egg and 1/4 cup of bread crumbs to the hamburger before forming into patties.

Try any of the following filling combinations:

Cooked chopped spinach and sauteed mushrooms
Sauteed mushrooms and onions
Cooked chopped spinach and sauteed onions
Your favorite sliced cheese
Thin slices of ham and cheese
Thin slices of ham, cheese, and cooked chopped spinach

Sliced cheese and green hot chile peppers

Use your imagination. Try anything you really like as a stuffing.

Cook your stuffed hamburger steak exactly as you would cook a steak, but for less time.

Top your stuffed hamburger steak with a small amount of melted butter and garlic salt, or make this simple sweet and sour glaze:

2 T. vinegar	2 T. water
2 bouillon cubes	dash of Worcestershire sauce
1/4 cup brown sugar	salt and pepper to taste

Bring to boil and simmer slowly for 10 minutes. Add 2 T. butter and spoon sparingly over hamburgers just before removing from grill.

PORK AND SPINACH PATTIES

1/2 lb. lean ground pork
1 small onion, chopped
1/2 cup bread crumbs
1 egg
1 lb. ground chuck
1 cup fresh spinach, chopped fine
1/4 cup red wine
salt and pepper
1 T. olive oil
2 T. Worcestershire sauce
1/2 cup catsup

Fry the pork and onion until the pork is crumbly. Mix the bread crumbs and egg well. Combine pork, egg mixture, ground chuck, wine and salt and pepper. Form into six large patties. Cook over low fire, about 45 minutes. Baste with sauce made with oil, Worcestershire sauce, and catsup. Serves 6. Serve on hamburger buns.

LAMB PATTIES

2 lbs. lean ground lamb
3 T. lime juice
1 tsp. salt
1 T. crushed coriander seeds
1 tsp. powdered saffron
1/4 cup cashew nuts, crushed
1/4 cup yoghurt

Put lime juice, salt, coriander seeds and saffron in a blender. Blend briefly and add cashews and yoghurt. Blend until smooth. Combine with lamb and mix thoroughly. Form into 8 patties and chill. Place on greased grill and cook until done. Do not overcook lamb; it should still be pink in the center. Serves 8.

VENISON BURGERS

2 lbs. ground venison
2 lbs. ground chuck
8 slices American cheese
1 can mushrooms
1 medium sized onion, chopped
2 T. butter
salt and pepper
garlic powder
8 strips bacon

Mix the venison and ground chuck well. Form into 16 large patties. Saute onion in butter. On half of the patties, place a slice of cheese, some mushrooms and onion, and seasoning. Top each with another patty and seal edges. Wrap a strip of bacon around each one and secure with a toothpick. Cook over medium-hot coals for about 10 minutes on each side. Serves 8.

HOT DOGS

Hot dogs are easy and fun. The kids love them so they are perfect for a family barbecue. They are not as economical as everyone seems to think but, served on a bun, they are certainly filling. There is no better way to cook hot dogs then to grill them, either whole or split, over charcoal. (A moderate fire is best to prevent bursting and curling.) They are tasty as they are, or can be dressed up with stuffings or sauces.

Cooking of delicate sausages such as bratwurst or bockwurst takes more care than the grilling of plain American hot dogs. They must be cooked gently and thoroughly. When cooking on your barbecue grill you must be sure to turn them frequently. Use tongs, not a fork. (You don't want to puncture the skins and lose the juices.) Your coals should be very low. I recommend that you precook them before placing them on the grill. Just put them in enough water to cover them, bring to a boil, and remove from the heat.

If the sausages do split while cooking, don't get excited. Just put some light type cheese in the cavity and go on as if nothing happened. Everybody will think you planned it that way.

COCKTAIL FRANKS

1 can tiny hot dogs
1/2 cup chili sauce
1 T. Worcestershire sauce
3 drops Tabasco
1 T. minced onion
pepper

   Combine ingredients for the sauce. Skewer the franks and brush them with sauce before placing on grill. Serve hot with the sauce as a dip. These can be cooked easily on a small hibachi. Or simply place some wire mesh over the grill on your large barbecue. You can add variety by alternating tiny onions or mushrooms with the franks.

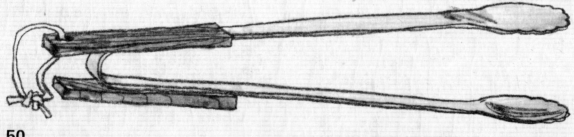

KRAUTDOGS

8 fat hot dogs
8 hot dog buns
2 cups sauerkraut

2 T. brown sugar
brown mustard

Split the hot dogs almost all the way through. Grill on both sides. While these are cooking, heat sauerkraut to which brown sugar has been added. When done, place hot dogs on buns that have been toasted over the coals. Place a scoop of sauerkraut on each and serve with brown mustard.

STUFFED FRANKS

6 hot dogs
6 slices bacon

2 T. grated cheddar cheese
2 T. minced onion

Split the hot dogs lengthwise, 3/4 of the way through, cutting almost to the ends. Combine cheese and onion and stuff in hot dogs. Wrap each with a slice of bacon and secure each end with a toothpick. Grill over coals until cheese starts melting and bacon is crisp, about 15 minutes. These can be served in a bun or alone.

LAMB

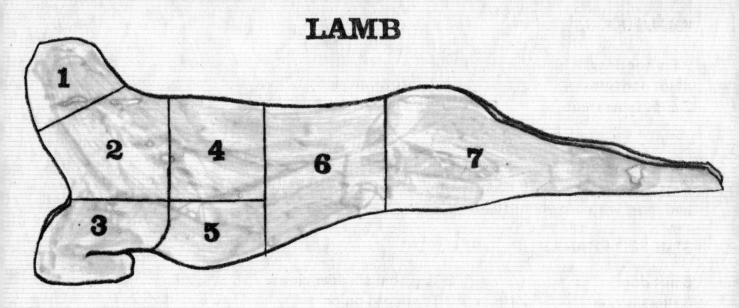

1. NECK   5. BREAST

2. SHOULDER   6. LOIN

3. SHANK   7. LEG

4. RIB

LAMB

Almost all countries have their favorite lamb recipes. Greeks season lamb with olive oil, lemon, and oregano. Indians prefer the sweet and hot flavors of cinnamon, coriander, and cumin. In Turkey lamb is usually prepared with a hint of fresh mint.

Lamb is perfectly suited for cooking over the coals. It's both tender and succulent. Almost all cuts are suitable for barbecuing, whether on the grill or on a rotisserie. Of course the most popular lamb dish for outdoor cooking is shish kabob, skewered chucks of juicy lamb cooked with a variety of vegetables.

The following cuts are best suited for regular barbecuing. In the case of roasts, you should choose cuts that have a small proportion of bone to meat. (However, it is possible to bone any of them and have a delicious rolled lamb roast.)

For barbecuing you will get the best results with a chop that is from 1 to 2-1/2 inches thick.

RACK OF LAMB

One rack of lamb will generally feed two people. When it is dressed up with paper frills, it makes an elegant main course. Its flavor is delicate and its texture very fine.

LOIN ROAST

The loin roast can be barbecued whole, or may be boned and rolled.

SIRLOIN ROAST

A sirloin is the upper part of the leg. You might have seen one at your butcher's as part of a full-cut leg of lamb. It usually weighs about 2 lbs. and is perfect for 2 people.

LEG OF LAMB

This is, of course, best for the rotisserie, but it can be boned and halved and laid on your grill. A leg of lamb roast usually weighs from 7 to 8 lbs. so it is a good cut for a family barbecue or a small gathering.

CHOPS

Any of the chops are tender enough to barbecue. But since the perfect lamb chop is crisp on the outside and still pink and juicy inside, you will get the best results with thick chops. The rib chop is perhaps the one you are most familiar with but it is generally too thin for barbecuing. Choose from among the round bone chop, the Saratoga, the boneless blade (often what is cut up and sold in your market as shish kabob), shoulder block (very thick, a double chop), or small loin chop.

Lamb is best when it is pink inside, so be careful not to overcook it. For medium-rare the thermometer will read 150°, medium 160°, and well-done (if you must!) about 170°.

Remember, always cook lamb uncovered. If you have an oven-type barbecue, do not close that lid unless you have good interior ventilation. I don't know what it is but there is something about lamb that needs to "escape" before lamb is at its best.

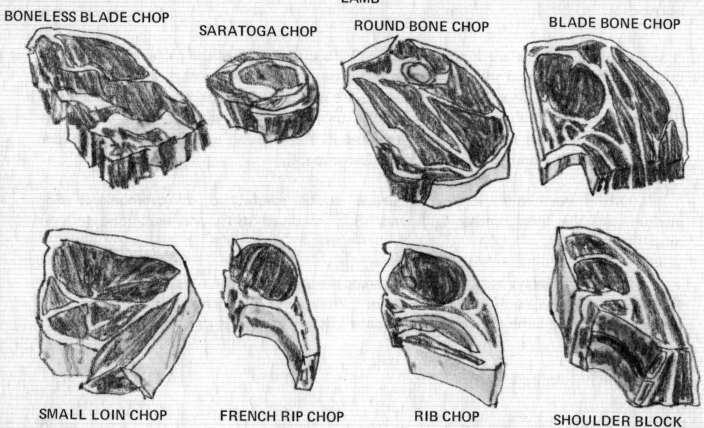

LAMB

BONELESS BLADE CHOP

SARATOGA CHOP

ROUND BONE CHOP

BLADE BONE CHOP

SMALL LOIN CHOP

FRENCH RIP CHOP

RIB CHOP

SHOULDER BLOCK

RACK OF LAMB WITH HERB SAUCE

2 seven rib racks of lamb
Sauce:
3/4 cup sherry
1 tsp. lemon juice
1 T. minced parsley
2 T. melted butter

1 tsp. grated onion
1 tsp. salt
dash pepper
1/2 tsp. dried rosemary
1/2 tsp. crushed oregano

Mix the ingredients for the sauce ahead of time. Trim off some but not all of the fat from the fatty side of the lamb rack and marinate for about 2 hours. Balance roasts on your spit. Use a weight if necessary to correct for any imbalance. Place a thermometer in the flesh of one of the racks, being careful that the tip does not touch bone or the spit. The coals should be hot and should be arranged around a drip pan that is placed directly under the meat. Cook for about 1-1/4 hours or until thermometer reads 160°. Baste frequently with herb sauce. Be sure you do not overcook. Lamb should be served still pink. Serves 4.

GARLIC LEG OF LAMB

6 lb. leg of lamb
salt and pepper
1/3 cup strong coffee
5 cloves garlic, peeled
1 tsp. grated lemon peel

Insert cloves of garlic in the leg of lamb by cutting little pockets in it with your paring knife. Rub with salt and pepper. Place over indirect heat. Cover and smoke about 2 hours. Heat coffee, butter, and lemon peel and use this as a baste while cooking. Use your thermometer to judge doneness. Serves 6-8.

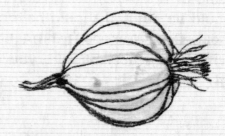

BASQUE LAMB BARBECUE

2 slices bacon, chopped
1 medium onion, finely chopped
1 boned leg of lamb, 7-8 lbs.
Marinade:
1 tsp. basil
1 tsp. oregano
2 tsp. olive oil

1/2 cup sherry
Basting sauce:
1/2 cup catsup
1/4 cup wine vinegar
1 small can tomato paste
1 cup dry white wine

Mix marinade of herbs, olive oil, and sherry. Marinate leg of lamb in the refrigerator all day, turning from time to time. Drain, saving marinade. Add basting sauce ingredients to excess marinade and simmer for 5 minutes. Saute onion and bacon. Sprinkle on lamb before rolling. Fold roast into a shape that is easy to handle, tucking in ends. Tie securely with string. Skewer and place over hot coals for about 1-1/2 hours or until thermometer indicates that it is done. Baste often. Serves 8.

BUTTERFLIED LEG OF LAMB WITH STUFFED MUSHROOMS

1 boned leg of lamb, 6 lbs.
10 large mushrooms
1 cup olive oil
2/3 cup dry red wine
1/4 tsp. thyme

1/2 tsp. oregano
1 tsp. salt
1/4 tsp. pepper
1 large onion, chopped
1/2 cup butter

Slice the thick portions of the lamb so that it will lie flat. Break the stems from the mushrooms and spoon out some of the "meat". Be careful not to break the skin. Marinate the lamb and mushroom caps in a mixture of olive oil, wine, thyme, oregano, salt, and pepper. Chop up mushroom stems and "meat" and combine with onion. Melt butter and add mushrooms and onion. Cook until tender. Remove meat from marinade and put on the grill, fat side down, over medium-hot coals for 45 minutes. Baste with marinade and turn occasionally. Fifteen minutes before lamb is done, drain mushroom caps and place cup side down on the grill for 5 minutes. Turn and spoon onion-mushroom mixture into caps. Cook 10 minutes. Serve stuffed mushrooms with hot, sliced lamb. Serves 6.

60

LAMB SHANKS

6 lbs. shanks
Marinade:
1 cup orange juice
1/2 cup lemon juice
2 T. sugar
1/2 cup fresh mint leaves, crushed
1/4 cup olive oil

Marinate shanks for at least 12 hours. During the last 2 hours, add mint. Oil the meat well and place on the grill over a slow fire and cook until thoroughly browned. Heat marinade and serve as a sauce with the meat. Serves 4.

GRILLED LAMB CHOPS, GREEK STYLE

4 lamb chops 1 to 1 1/2 inches thick
2/3 cup olive oil
2/3 cup lemon juice
1 medium-sized onion, chopped
1 tsp. salt
1 tsp. oregano
dash pepper
parsley sprigs
lemon slices
onion slices

Marinate lamb chops in olive oil, lemon juice, onion, salt, oregano, and pepper 4 to 5 hours. Drain meat. Grill over very hot coals 5 to 6 minutes on each side or until done, basting with marinade. Garnish with parsley, lemon, and onion slices. Will serve 4 to 6, depending on size of chops.

ARMENIAN SHISH KABOB

4 lbs. boneless blade chops
Marinade:
1/2 tsp. minced parsley
1 tsp. marjoram
1 tsp. cumin
1 tsp. salt
1 tsp. ground pepper
1 green pepper, finely chopped
1 onion, finely chopped
1/2 cup lemon juice
1 cup tomato juice
1/2 cup dill pickle juice

Cut meat into cubes. Combine ingredients for the marinade and pour over lamb. Marinate for 5 hours. Salt the meat. Skewer and broil over medium coals until done. Baste frequently with remaining marinade. Serves 6. For more shish kabob recipes, see SKEWER COOKING.

BASIC LAMB SAUCE

3/4 cup sherry
1 slice lemon
1 sprig parsley
2 T. olive oil
1 tsp. grated onion
1 tsp. salt
1/2 tsp. pepper
1 sprig fresh rosemary or 1/2 tsp. dried rosemary
1 sprig oregano or 1/2 tsp. dried oregano

Mix ingredients and let stand for several hours to allow flavor to blend. Sauce can be used with any cut of lamb you choose. Use as a marinade and a baste. Heat and serve as a sauce.

BARBECUED LAMB CHOPS

6 thick lamb chops
1/3 cup beer
1/3 cup tomato juice
2 T. cider vinegar
1/2 tsp. white pepper
1/4 tsp. salt
1 small onion (finely chopped)
1 clove garlic, crushed
1 tsp. dry mustard
1/4 cup Worcestershire sauce

Mix all ingredients together and marinate lamb chops for 3 hours at room temperature (or overnight). Barbecue the chops about 7" from a solid bed of hot coals until done. Heat marinade and pour over the chops and arrange on a serving platter.

PORK

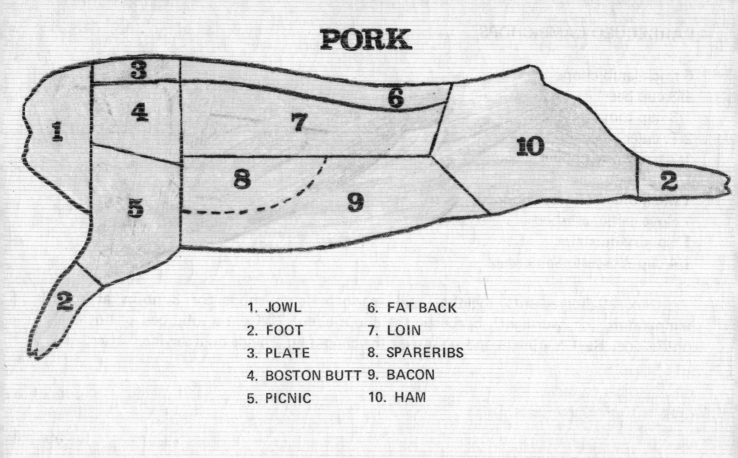

1. JOWL
2. FOOT
3. PLATE
4. BOSTON BUTT
5. PICNIC

6. FAT BACK
7. LOIN
8. SPARERIBS
9. BACON
10. HAM

PORK

Although most pork is government inspected, it is still necessary to cook it completely. This doesn't mean overdone. The best results are obtained with long, low, even temperatures. An interior heat of 175° or 180° after a suitable period of time will achieve good juicy results. For instance, a 12 lb. spit roasted fresh ham (not smoked) will take about 4 hours. (After cooking, let the roast "rest" for several minutes before serving.) A covered barbecue is good for these long cooking times. If you stuff a pork roast, keep the stuffing on the dry side. There's plenty of juice available in the meat. Make sure your coals are not directly under the pork when cooking, because it drips more fat than most meats. A drip-pan or some foil will serve on clean-up too. Here's a good sauce for charcoaled pork:

1 2/3 cups fresh orange juice
1/3 cup lemon juice
1/3 cup olive oil
1 1/2 tsp. rosemary
black pepper to taste
drop or two of lime juice

SIRLOIN PORK ROAST

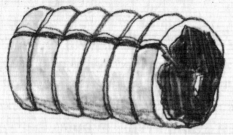

PORK

SALT PORK

BLADE PORK STEAKS

LOIN CHOP

FRENCHED RIP CHOP

CANADIAN BACON

BUTTERFLY CHOP

RIP PORK CHOP

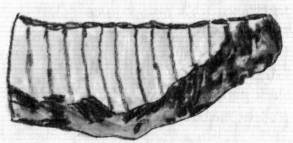

SPARE RIPS

PINEAPPLE SPARERIBS FOR 10

10 lbs. spareribs
12 peppercorns
6 whole cloves
2 bay leaves
2 cloves garlic

Sweet and sour sauce:
1 can (8 1/2 oz.) crushed pineapple, undrained
3/4 cup dry white wine
3 T. wine vinegar
2 T. olive oil
1 T. soy sauce
1 T. chopped onion
1 T. brown sugar
1 tsp. lemon juice
1/2 tsp. garlic salt

Place ribs, peppercorns, cloves, bay leaves, garlic in a large pot and cover with water. Simmer for about 30 minutes. Cool and refrigerate until time of your barbecue. Combine all sauce ingredients, bring to a boil and simmer for 15 minutes. Place ribs on grill over medium coals. Baste with sauce.

BUTTERFLIED PORK ROAST

1 pork butt, boned and butterflied
Marinade:
1/4 tsp. pepper
1 1/2 tsp. salt
1/4 cup olive oil
1/2 cup vinegar
1/3 cup chopped parsley
2 cloves garlic, minced

Place fatty side of meat on your chopping board and score with 1/2-inch deep cuts both lengthwise and crosswise. Place in a baking dish and cover with marinade. Let set for 3 hours. Place meat, scored side down, over low heat and cook for 1 hour. Turn meat and cook for another hour. Baste frequently with marinade. Slice and serve. Serves 12.

LEMON SPARERIBS

4 lbs. pork spareribs
1 lemon sliced thin
1 onion sliced thin
salt and pepper to taste

Salt and pepper ribs. Place on grill and cook one side thoroughly. Turn ribs and place slices of onion and lemon on them. Cook until done. Remove lemon and onion, cut apart and serve. Serves 4.

SPARERIBS SUPREME

4 lbs. spareribs
1 onion, diced
2 cups diced celery
3 T. butter
2 cups tomato sauce
2 tsp. prepared mustard
2 T. brown sugar
2 T. lemon juice

2 T. liquid smoke
2 T. vinegar
1 T. salt
1/4 tsp. pepper
6 drops Tabasco
1/2 cup water
2 T. chili powder
1/2 tsp. ground cloves

Melt butter in large frying pan and add onion and celery, browning them lightly.

Add remaining ingredients and bring to boil. Reduce heat and simmer for 1/2 hour. Refrigerate until ready to use. Place spareribs on grill and cook until done, basting frequently with sauce. Cut into serving pieces. Serves 6.

PORK ROAST WITH MELON

4 lb. rolled loin pork roast
3 cantaloupes
2 small packages cream cheese with chives
1/2 cup cream

Place roast on skewer or on grill in covered barbecue. Cook for 2 hours or until done. Whip cream and fold in cream cheese with chives. Peel canteloupes and cut into 1/2 inch thick rings. Cut barbecued roast into 8 thick slices and place on top of each melon ring. Top with spoonful of cheese and cream mixture. Serves 8.

PORK WITH PEANUT BUTTER AND ORANGE JUICE

5-6 lbs. pork loins, boned
1/4 cup peanut butter, creamy style
1/2 cup orange juice

    With fat side out, tie pork loins together to form a rolled roast. They should overlap at 2 inch intervals. Balance on spit with holding forks. Sprinkle with salt and pepper. Push coals to back of barbecue and place drip pan under roast. While roast is turning on spit, cover. Allow about 3-4 hours cooking time. Insert meat thermometer. When roast is almost done, brush on peanut butter and orange juice combination and continue cooking and basting for 15 minutes. Serves 10.

GRILLED CANADIAN BACON

1 1/2 lbs. Canadian bacon, in one piece
1 T. brown sugar
1/4 cup orange juice
1 tsp. ground cloves

Make a sauce of the brown sugar, orange juice and cloves. In 1/2-inch grill pattern, score surface of bacon with knife. Place meat on grill 4 inches from medium-hot coals, baste meat often. Cook 40-45 minutes, turning frequently.

WILD GAME

Preparation of wild game is very little different from the preparation of other meats, except that some wild meats have a strong "gamey" flavor which needs masking. Marinades are the ideal way of flavoring game, and the following recipes make good use of them.

VENISON STEAK

8 6-oz. venison steaks, 1 inch thick
1/4 cup lemon juice
1/4 cup wine vinegar
1/3 cup salad oil
2/3 cup olive oil
1 1/2 tsp. unseasoned meat tenderizer
4 loaves French bread (1/2 lb. size)

1 large onion, thinly sliced
2 cloves garlic, finely chopped
1 cup parsley, finely chopped
1/2 tsp. dried thyme leaves
1 tsp. sugar
1/4 tsp. pepper

Bring steak to room temperature and lay in shallow dish, sprinkling both sides with meat tenderizer. In covered jar combine and mix all ingredients except onion by shaking well. Marinate steak in this mixture one hour. Wrap bread loaves individually in foil, placing on grill for 20 minutes to warm. Grill venison 4 inches from coals, 5 minutes on each side for medium. Lay steaks on bottom half of bread loaves cut lengthwise, covering with onion and top half of loaf. To serve cut bread in half crosswise. Serves 8.

ELK STEAK-HUNTER STYLE

Elk steak, 2-2 1/2 inches thick
1/2 tsp. onion salt
1/4 tsp. celery salt
1/4 tsp. garlic salt
1/2 tsp. chili powder
1/4 tsp. salt
1/4 tsp. pepper
quilted broiling foil

Prepare and cool meat 24 hours before dividing into individual steaks. Wiping meat clean with damp cloth, sprinkle both sides with above spices and let stand 45 minutes at room temperature. In large skillet prepare the following sauce by simmering over a low fire:
Sauce:
1/4 cup pineapple juice
4 T. olive oil

2 tsp. vinegar
1 tsp. celery salt
1 tsp. chili powder
1/2 tsp. pepper
1/2 tsp. salt
1/2 cup brown sugar
1 T. Worcestershire sauce

1 tsp. garlic salt

1 tsp. onion salt
1/2 pint water
1 15-oz. can tomato sauce

Broil meat until lightly brown on each side (20 minutes) over low and evenly distributed coals. Broil another 45 minutes to an hour wrapped in quilted broiling foil, opening, basting and turning every 15 minutes. Serve with remaining sauce over meat.

GRILLED RABBIT

1 domestic rabbit, dressed and cut into serving pieces
Tabasco sauce
Basting Sauce:
1/2 cup water
juice from 1 lemon
1/8 tsp. each: cinnamon, allspice, onion salt
1/2 tsp. pulverized dried mint leaves

1 T. dried parsley
1/2 tsp. paprika
1/4 tsp. pepper
1 tsp. salt
4 T. kirsch
1/2 cup butter
juice of 1 orange

Sprinkle rabbit with Tabasco sauce and let stand. Simmer all ingredients for basting sauce in saucepan (except butter and brandy) 5 minutes, and pour over rabbit. Simmer basting sauce 2-3 minutes after draining from rabbit and adding butter and brandy. Keep warm on back of grill, while basting pieces of rabbit generously and often until tender (1 hour). Outside will burn easily if allowed to dry out. Meaty side should be grilled facing upwards first.

BROILED QUAIL

Quail comes in a wide range of sizes, depending on the part of the country they come from. You will have to estimate the number you need based upon the size of the quail available. A whole quail is usually spit roasted, but for this recipe you can use your grill.

Clean the quail. Chop the giblets and saute in butter that has been flavored with just a little rum. Keep warm. Split quail with your cleaver. Broil over hot coals for 8-10 minutes, basting frequently and generously with melted butter. Cook until skin is crisp. Spread the sauteed giblets on toast and place quail on top.

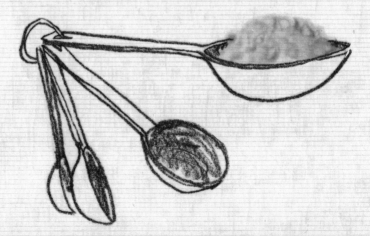

SEAFOOD

Barbecuing fish is easy, economical, and fun. There are just a few rules to learn which will help you to get perfect results every time.

Always use fresh fish. If the eyes are bright and the flesh moist and firm, it's fresh. The gills should not be too dark in color and the fishy odor should be slight. If you use frozen fish, it should be completely thawed before cooking. Grilling a partially thawed fish will overcook it on the outside, leaving the middle underdone.

Never overcook fish. It ruins its naturally sweet, delicate flavor. Most fish will flake easily at the gentle touch of a fork when done. Better to undercook a little and return it to the grill.

When preparing seafood steaks, fillets, kabobs, etc., try to have the rest of the dinner almost ready. Because of the short cooking time, the above cuts will need most of your attention. I always have a heavy, hot metal serving dish ready so the fish will remain warm on the table as long as possible. Fish is at its best when hot and fresh from the broiler.

Be careful when handling fish, particularly if a marinade has been used. Marinades weaken fish. Use of a rack, frame, or a hinged wire broiler is advisable.

Always oil the grill, rack, foil, etc. Otherwise the fish will stick and may come apart.

Handle the fish as little as possible, especially when it's on the grill. Don't turn it any more than is necessary. Use a sharp-edged thin spatula to lift the fish carefully, turn gently and replace. Once you get the hang of it, one turn per fish steak should do it. Just remember, the thicker cuts of fish will take longer than the thin. Allow about 7 minutes total cooking time for a 1-inch steak or fillet, about 15 minutes for a 2-inch cut.

Your fire should not be too hot. Keep it moderate, especially when cooking a large, whole fish, such as salmon or barracuda. Try not to drip butter into the fire to avoid flare ups.

A good trick when broiling fish is to sprinkle some herbs, such as thyme, dill, or fennel, on the coals. Or use a personal mixture of your favorites. If you do use herbs for the smoke, keep the baste simple. Just butter with a hint of lemon, for example. The herb flavor will be very subtle.

If you are lucky enough to catch a large salmon and you want to display the entire fish, you might want to serve it with the head and tail on, however, it is necessary to cover them with foil to protect them from the heat. Then cover the entire fish with wire cloth. This will make it much easier to handle. If you want to cook a large fish on a rotating spit, it's wise to use a commercial fish rack that is made for this purpose.

Cooking fish in open tubs of foil works well, particularly with fish pieces or marinated fish. Completely enclosing fish in foil will result in baked or steamed fish. Most oven recipes can be converted for outdoor cooking by this method. Remember, have a good-sized moderate fire going. Oil the foil well and turn often. If your barbecue has a hood that closes completely, so much the better. Fish cooked in this way can really be improved by the flambe process. Put the cooked fish in a shallow plate (metal, if you have it). Add some fresh herbs on the top. Pour over a couple jiggers of cognac and light. Really effective for the special evening cookout.

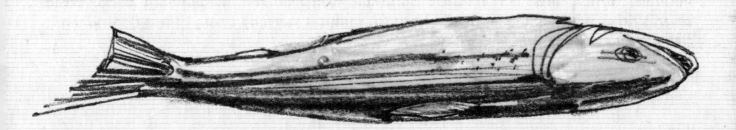

MARINATED SALMON STEAKS

2 lbs. salmon steaks
Marinade:
1 cup oil and vinegar dressing
1 T. lemon juice
1 tsp. paprika
salt and pepper

Make an oil and vinegar salad dressing with no seasoning. Combine with lemon juice, paprika, salt and pepper. Dip steaks in cold, salted water and pat dry. Marinate for 30 minutes, turning after 15 minutes. Barbecue 4 inches over medium-hot coals. Baste several times with marinade. Cook about 10 minutes, turning once. Fish is done when it flakes easily with a fork. Serves 6-8.

GRILLED SWORDFISH STEAKS

2 large swordfish steaks, cut in half
Marinade:
1/2 cup soy sauce
1/4 cup catsup
1/4 cup chopped parsley
1/2 cup orange juice
2 garlic cloves, mashed
2 T. lemon juice
1 tsp. pepper

Marinate swordfish for 1 hour in marinade. Grill about 4 inches above hot coals for 15 minutes, turning once. Baste frequently while cooking. Serves 4.

COGNAC BARBECUED STRIPED BASS

4 large striped bass steaks
Marinade:
2 T. soy sauce
1/2 cup cognac
1/4 cup melted butter
2 T. lemon juice

    Dip steaks in cold, salted water and pat dry. Marinate in lemon juice, soy sauce, cognac, and melted butter for 1 hour. Grill 4 inches above hot coals for about 12 minutes, turning once. Baste frequently while cooking. Serves 6.

WINE BARBECUED SEA BASS

2 lbs. sea bass fillet
Marinade:
1/2 onion, chopped
1 garlic clove, minced
1/2 cup butter
1 8-oz. can tomato sauce
2 T. sherry
1/2 tsp. sugar
1 tsp. Worcestershire sauce
salt and pepper
pinch each thyme and oregano

Saute onion and garlic in butter until tender. Cool and combine with remaining marinade ingredients. Dip fish fillets in cold, salted water and pat dry. Marinate for 1 hour. Cook 4 inches from coals, about 5 minutes on each side. Baste frequently. Serves 6.

BROILED FILLET OF PERCH

2 lbs. fillet of perch
Marinade:
1/2 cup frozen lemonade concentrate
1/2 cup catsup
1/2 cup melted butter
2 T. capers and sauce
4 bay leaves, crushed
1 garlic clove, minced
1 tsp. prepared mustard
salt and pepper

Dip fillets in salted cold water and pat dry. Cut into serving pieces and marinate for 30 minutes. Drain. Barbecue 4 inches above hot coals, basting often with marinade. Cook about 15 minutes, turning once. Serves 6.

HICKORY SMOKED FILLETS

2 lbs. fish fillets
Baste:
2 T. lemon juice
1/2 cup melted butter
pinch garlic powder
1 T. chopped parsley
salt and pepper

Combine ingredients for baste. Dip fish fillets in salted, cold water and pat dry. Put water-soaked hickory chips on the fire. Barbecue 4 inches above hot coals for 10 minutes, turning once and basting often. Serves 6.

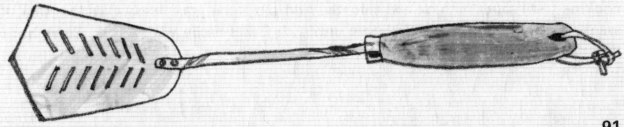

TROUT WITH CAPER SAUCE

6 1-lb. rainbow or brook trout
Sauce:
3 T. butter
3 T. flour
3/4 cup hot water
3/4 cup hot beer
1/2 tsp. salt
1/2 cup capers
1 T. chopped parsley
juice of 1 lime

Melt butter in a pan and stir in the flour. Add beer and water gradually, stirring and cooking until sauce is thick and smooth. Add salt, lime juice, capers, and parsley. Keep warm. Split and grill trout. Barbecue until fish flakes easily with a fork. Serve hot with accompanying sauce. Serves 6.

FOIL-BARBECUED SMELT

6 whole smelt
6 strips bacon, diced
1 T. lemon juice
1 T. chopped parsley
pinch garlic powder
salt and pepper
lemon wedges

Dip smelt in cold, salted water and pat dry. Fry bacon, parsley and onion lightly. Stir in lemon juice, salt, pepper, and garlic powder. Place smelt in center of piece of aluminum foil, well greased. Rub each fish with bacon mixture and place remaining seasonings in cavities. Wrap in foil, sealing the edges. Set packages in medium coals. Cook 15 minutes, turning a few times with tongs. Serve garnished with lemon wedges. Serves 6.

ABALONE AND ALMOND BUTTER

2 lbs. abalone
1/4 lb. melted butter
1 T. lemon juice
1/2 cup toasted sliced almonds

    Pound abalone between two pieces of wax paper until thin, or have it done for you at the fish market.

    Barbecue about 5 inches from hot coals, basting often with lemon butter. Abalone cooks very fast; 2 to 3 minutes on each side should do it. Add almonds to remaining butter in pan. Serve by pouring lemon and almonds over each serving. Serves 4.

STUFFED FLOUNDER

5 medium-sized flounders
1 onion, chopped
1/2 green pepper, chopped
2 slices bacon, diced
1 lb. crab meat
2 cups bread crumbs

3 eggs
salt and pepper
3/4 cup butter
1 tsp. salt
1 tsp. paprika
1 T. lemon juice

Wash fish in cold salted water. Cut a slit down the center of the broad side. Run a knife between the ribs and the flesh to make a pocket. Saute onion and green pepper with bacon until bacon is crisp. Add crab meat, bread crumbs, beaten eggs, and salt and pepper to taste. Stuff flounder with this mixture.

Melt the butter and add the salt, paprika, and lemon juice. Lay each fish on a square of heavy duty aluminum foil, large enough to completely wrap around the fish. Pour some of the butter on each, turning the fish to butter both sides. Wrap each fish securely and place on the grill over medium-hot coals. Cook 20-30 minutes.

BARBECUED SCALLOPS

1 1/2 lbs. sea scallops
Marinade:
3/4 cup melted butter
2 T. lemon juice
1/2 tsp. onion salt
1/8 tsp. garlic salt
salt and pepper
paprika

Wash scallops in cold, salted water and pat dry. Marinate for 1 hour. Place scallops in a well-greased hinged wire grill. Cook 4 inches above medium coals for 3-5 minutes on each side. Turn once and baste often. Scallops are done when they are nicely browned. Serves 6. (Scallops can also be wrapped in bacon and skewered for cooking.)

BROILED WHOLE LOBSTERS

This makes a truly elegant barbecue and it is very simple. Buy large lobsters, at least 1 1/4 lbs. Broil them over medium hot coals, turning from time to time. They will be done in about 12-14 minutes. Remove from the coals. Remove the stomach and fill with melted butter. Serve on heated plates. Have some melted butter to which you have added lemon juice on the table for individual use.

BROILED OYSTERS

1 quart oysters   beaten egg
melted butter   bread crumbs
pepper

Dry the oysters in a cloth. Dip each in peppered melted butter. Then dip them in beaten egg, then in bread crumbs. Broil on wire mesh for 3 to 5 minutes. Drip a little melted butter over them before serving. Serves 4.

BASTES FOR FISH

DRAWN BUTTER SAUCE

2 T. butter
3 T. flour
1/2 tsp. salt
1 tsp. lemon juice
dash white pepper
1 1/2 cups water
2 tsp. minced parsley

Melt 1 T. butter in a double boiler. Stir in flour, salt, and pepper. Add water gradually and stir until smooth. Cook 7-8 minutes, then stir in remaining butter and the lemon juice. Stir in parsley.

DRAWN BUTTER WITH ANCHOVY

Add 1 1/2 T. anchovy paste to your drawn butter recipe.

ALMOND BUTTER

1/2 cup butter
1 T. lemon juice
Almond extract to taste

Melt butter in a double boiler or over low heat in a saucepan. Add lemon juice and almond extract. This makes a good baste and a delicious sauce over fish. Sprinkle with shaved almonds.

SOY BUTTER

1/3 cup butter
1/3 cup soy sauce
2 cloves garlic, mashed
2 tsp. Worcestershire sauce

SAUCES FOR FISH

Tartar sauce is the best known and the most popular sauce to serve with fish. But there are countless others that you will no doubt want to try. Make several and let your guests choose their favorite or try them all.

TARTAR SAUCE

1 cup mayonnaise
1 T. minced onion
1 T. parsley
2 T. sweet pickle relish
1 tsp. garlic powder

Combine all ingredients and chill.

CURRY SAUCE

3 T. butter
3 T. flour
1 cup milk
2 T. curry powder

Melt butter in a saucepan. Add flour and stir until smooth. Add milk gradually and stir until you have a smooth, thick white sauce. Add curry powder. Taste and add more if you like.

CHEESE SAUCE

3 T. butter   salt and pepper
3 T. flour   1/2 cup grated cheddar cheese
1 cup milk

Melt butter in a saucepan. Add flour and stir until smooth. Gradually add milk, stirring constantly. When mixture is smooth, add cheese and stir until melted.

POULTRY

Chicken, turkey, duck and other fowl are at their best when barbecued. The smoke flavor penetrates the delicate meat in a way that most people find extremely pleasant. In fact, inexpensive poultry is so good barbecued, that it is the first choice for outdoor cooking of a large number of patio chefs.

The covered brazier makes the job practically foolproof. Just proceed as follows:

(1) Move all of the coals to one side of the unit, and place your chicken, duck or small turkey halves or parts on the other end of the grill. Open your vents wide, add a handful of wood chips and close the lid.

(2) In 15 minutes, baste the top side, add a few more chips and close the lid.

(3) In 15 more minutes baste the top side again, turn the pieces over and baste the other side and close the lid.

(4) In 30 more minutes, the meat should be done, and should be nicely browned. If it is not brown enough to suit you, move the pieces over the coals and brown them quickly on each side, and serve.

If you do not have a covered barbecue, simply brown both sides of the pieces about 4" above the coals. Then raise the grill and cook for about 25 minutes turning and basting frequently.

Large birds can be cooked whole either stuffed, or unstuffed, in the same way, either on a rotisserie or without one in the covered barbecue. In the uncovered barbecue, large birds must be cooked on the rotisserie, in which case, you cook them the same way you barbecue roast beef. Use a meat thermometer in either case to determine when meat is done.

The following recipes will add variety to your barbecue menus.

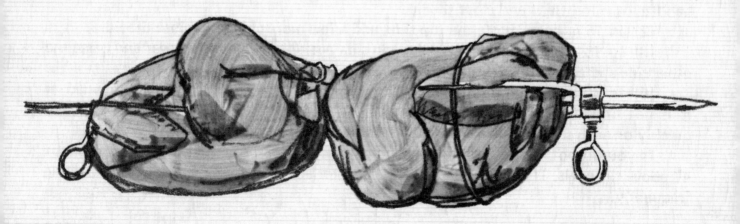

BARBECUED CHICKEN

For whole chicken, have your butcher split them and remove the backbone so that they will lie flat on the grill. Use small broiling chickens for this cooking method. If you buy large fryers, have them cut into serving pieces. Remember, use any of the following marinades for your split chicken, chicken pieces, or whole chickens.

SOUR CREAM MARINADE

1 cup sour cream
2 garlic cloves, mashed
1 tsp. Worcestershire sauce
1 T. lemon juice
1/2 tsp. salt
1/2 tsp. paprika
dash white pepper
dash celery salt

Combine all ingredients and pour over chicken. Refrigerate overnight before cooking.

WILD RICE STUFFED CORNISH HENS

6 thawed 1-lb. Rock Cornish hens
1 T. minced parsley
1/3 cup melted butter
1/2 cup soy sauce
salt

Wild rice stuffing:
1/3 cup wild rice
2 T. soft butter
2 T. blanched almonds, slivered and toasted
1/2 tsp. sage
1/4 cup golden raisins
salt to taste

Rinse rice and cook in boiling water until tender. Drain. Add butter, almonds, sage, raisins, and salt.

Rinse hens and pat dry. Put 1/4 cup stuffing in each hen. Truss and close cavity. Tie wings to body and legs to tail. Balance on spit and secure with holding forks or follow preceding instructions for covered units. Baste with soy sauce, parsley, and melted butter mixture from time to time. Roast over medium coals for 1 1/4 hours. Serves 6.

HERB BASTE

1/2 cup butter
dash dried savory
dash dried rosemary
dash dried thyme

Melt butter and add herbs. Let stand to allow the flavors to blend. Add more herbs if desired.

MUSTARD-HONEY BASTE

1/2 cup honey
1/4 cup prepared mustard
2 T. lemon juice
1 tsp. salt

Combine all ingredients in a bowl. Don't be stingy; baste frequently.

GREEK MARINADE

1/4 cup lemon juice
1 garlic clove, mashed
1/2 cup olive oil
1/2 tsp. pepper
1 tsp. salt

1 tsp. thyme
1 tsp. marjoram
1 small onion, chopped
1/4 cup minced parsley

Combine all ingredients and pour over chicken. Marinate overnight in refrigerator.

ROSEMARY MARINADE

1/4 cup olive oil
1/4 cup white wine vinegar
1/2 tsp. pepper

2 tsp. crushed fresh rosemary
1/2 onion, sliced

Combine all ingredients and let stand to blend flavors. Pour over chicken and refrigerate overnight.

ROCK CORNISH HENS WITH PINEAPPLE STUFFING

4 thawed 1-lb. Rock Cornish hens
1/2 cup melted butter
1 tsp. salt
2 1/2 T. lemon juice
1 1-lb. can pineapple chunks, drained

Rinse hens and pat dry. Lightly salt insides. Stuff with pineapple. Truss hens and close cavity. Tie wings to body and legs to tail. Balance on spit and secure with holding forks, or follow preceding instructions for covered units. Baste from time to time with mixture of salt, butter and lemon. Barbecue over medium coals for 1 1/4 hours. Serves 4.

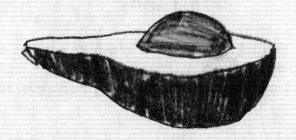

TARRAGON BASTE

1 cup firmly packed brown sugar
1/2 cup tarragon vinegar
2 T. butter

Combine ingredients in a saucepan. Stir and bring to a boil. Let stand to allow flavors to blend.

GRILLED CHICKEN BREASTS

4 large chicken breasts, split   3/4 cup flour
1/2 cup melted butter   salt and pepper

Dip chicken breasts in melted butter. Then shake in a paper bag of flour, salt and pepper. Have a hot fire going. Place chicken on greased grill and cook for about 10 minutes on each side. Baste from time to time with melted butter. Skin should be crispy. Serves 4.

CHICKEN WITH PEACHES

2 small chickens, cut up
Marinade:
1/2 cup lemon juice
2 T. honey
1/2 tsp. salt
1/2 cup melted butter
4 large peaches, peeled and halved

Mix together lemon juice, honey, and salt. Marinate chicken pieces in this mixture in the refrigerator for about 1 hour. Place chicken on grill over medium-hot coals. Cook for about 40 minutes, basting with marinade to which you have added melted butter. About 10 minutes before chicken is ready, dip peach halves in marinade and place on grill. Cook 10 minutes, basting frequently and turning once. Serve chicken on a platter surrounded by peaches. Serves 4.

BRANDIED CHICKEN

2 small chickens, split
salt and pepper
1 can red cherries
1 can apricot halves
Baste:
1/2 cup melted butter
1/4 cup lemon juice
1/4 cup brandy
1/4 cup firmly packed brown sugar

Sprinkle chicken with salt and pepper. Place on grill over medium hot fire. Cook for about 40 minutes, basting from time to time. Place cherries and apricots in a shallow foil pan 10 minutes before chicken is done. Pour a little of the basting sauce over the fruit. The grill should be covered at all times except when you are basting. Serve chicken on a platter with fruit poured over. Serves 4.

ORANGE BAKED CHICKEN

1 3-lb. chicken, cut up
salt and pepper
4 T. orange juice concentrate, thawed
4 T. butter

Divide chicken in 4 serving portions. Place on 4 pieces of heavy duty foil large enough to wrap completely and sprinkle each with salt and pepper. Pour 1 T. orange juice concentrate and place 1 T. butter on each. Wrap securely in foil and bake in or over hot coals for about 1 hour. Serves 4.

113

CHICKEN TANDOORI

1 3-lb. chicken, quartered
2 cups yoghurt
4 garlic cloves, mashed
3 T. butter
3 bay leaves, crumbled
salt to taste
1 tsp. cayenne pepper
1/2 tsp. powdered cardamom
1 tsp. powdered cinnamon
1/2 tsp. powdered cloves
1 tsp. powdered ginger
1 tsp. curry powder

Prick chicken pieces all over with a fork and marinate for 5 hours in a combination of yoghurt and garlic. Turn often. Mix remaining ingredients. Rub this paste on chicken and let stand for 2-3 hours. Barbecue over medium coals for 45-55 minutes. Serves 4.

SPANISH STYLE CHICKEN

1 3-lb. chicken, quartered
1/4 lb. butter
1 garlic clove, mashed
3/4 tsp. salt
3/4 tsp. savory
1/2 tsp. paprika
dash cinnamon
dash crushed tarragon

Melt butter. Add garlic, salt, savory, paprika, cinnamon, and tarragon. Place chicken on barbecue grill over medium coals. Baste frequently with butter. Cook about 45 minutes. Serve chicken over hot rice that has been seasoned with the basting butter. Serves 4.

MUSHROOM STUFFING

1 lb. fresh mushrooms, sliced
1/4 lb. butter
1/2 onion, chopped
4 cups soft bread crumbs
1/4 tsp. pepper
1/2 tsp. sage
2/3 cup chicken or beef broth

Saute mushrooms for 5 minutes in a large skillet of 3 T. butter. Spoon out mushrooms into a large bowl, add 1 T. more butter. Saute onions until clear but not brown. Melt remaining butter and add it to mushrooms and onions. Mix well with bread crumbs, pepper and sage. Spoon broth over the mixture and mix gently. Makes enough to stuff a medium-sized chicken. Double the recipe for turkey. Mushroom stuffing can also be used for beef.

CELERY-CARROT STUFFING

1 cup sifted flour
1 tsp. baking powder
1/2 tsp. nutmeg
1/2 tsp. salt
1/2 cup chopped pecans
1/2 cup wheat germ
1 cup bread crumbs, lightly browned in butter

1/4 cup butter
1/2 cup brown sugar
1 egg
1 cup shredded carrots
1/4 cup chopped celery
3 T. chopped parsley

Sift flour with nutmeg, baking powder and salt. Stir in nuts, wheat germ and crumbs. Cream butter and blend with brown sugar. Add egg and mix well. Add carrots, parsley and celery. Add sifted dry ingredients and stir lightly. This makes enough to stuff a medium-sized chicken.

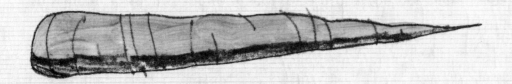

YAM STUFFING

1 large onion, minced
1/2 green pepper, minced
2 T. butter
2 large tomatoes, peeled, seeded and diced
12 cooked yams, peeled
salt and pepper
1/2 tsp. poultry seasoning
1 egg, well beaten
3 T. cream

In a large frying pan, saute onion and green pepper in melted butter until onion is just yellow. Add tomatoes and stew for 5-6 minutes or until juices have evaporated. Add yams, which have been cut into small pieces. Season with salt, pepper and poultry seasoning to taste. Let cool. Then add egg and cream. Makes about 6 cups or enough to stuff a 5-6 lb. chicken.

TURKEY

Turkey is generally cooked on a rotating spit because of its size. However, if you do not have a rotisserie, and your oven is small, you can have your butcher cut up a turkey and grill the pieces.

You can use the barbecue sauce for either spit roasted or grilled turkey. Basting with plain melted butter, especially for a stuffed turkey, is simple and delicious.

GRILLED TURKEY PIECES

Buy a 6-7 lb. turkey to serve from 10 to 12 people. Have your butcher cut it for you or cut it yourself as follows: 2 wings, 2 thighs, 2 drumsticks, 4 breast pieces, and 2 back pieces. Start your coals early so that you have a good, steady medium-hot fire. The grill should be about 7 inches above the coals. Cook, turning and basting from time to time, for about 1 1/2 hours. The wings and back pieces should not be placed on the fire until the other pieces have cooked for 1/2 hour. Your turkey is done when there is no pinkness in the meat of the drumstick. Test by cutting open with a sharp knife.

SPIT ROASTED TURKEY

Start your coals early so that you have a slow and steady fire. It is best to place them toward the back of your rotisserie and have a drip pan directly under the turkey.

Sprinkle the inside of the bird with salt. The skewer should be inserted through the center of the neck skin to just above the tail. Insert the skewer forks into the breast and tail. Test for balance by rotating the skewer in your hands. Use a weight on your rotisserie to correct for any imbalance. This will insure even cooking of your turkey and will avoid strain on the motor. Use string or wire to secure the wings and the legs close to the body. Baste from time to time with melted butter and drippings. If you use the barbecue sauce, apply only during the last half hour of cooking. Use a thermometer for best results. This should be inserted into the thickest part of the thigh. Be sure the tip is not touching bone or your reading will not be accurate.

BARBECUE SAUCE

Again, plain melted butter is preferable for turkey. If you do choose to use this sauce, it also works well as a marinade for the cut-up turkey pieces. Marinate for about 2 hours at room temperature before cooking and use as a baste as well.

1/4 cup melted butter
1/4 cup soy sauce
1 T. orange marmalade
1 tsp. dry mustard
1 tsp. powdered ginger
1 clove garlic, mashed

VEGETABLES

You can take advantage of the hot coals you use to barbecue your main dish, to also cook an accompanying vegetable. Almost any vegetable can be barbecued. Familiar tastes take on a new and exciting aspect when cooked with charcoal, or, if you prefer, you can wrap your vegetable in foil to preserve more of its natural flavor.

Your choice of vegetable will, of course, depend upon the entree. Your cooking method might also be dictated by the way you are cooking your main dish. For example, if your grill is going to be completely covered with steaks, you could cook a vegetable skewered up above on the rotisserie, or wrapped in foil and placed directly on the coals. On the other hand, if you are using your rotisserie to roast a turkey, you can place the vegetables on the grill.

Vegetables that are cooking bare (without foil) should be basted frequently, whether they are being cooked on the rotisserie or directly on the grill. Melted butter with spices and herbs is best. Cooking time will vary, depending upon whether you are grilling green pepper strips or baking a potato. You might decide that you want to parboil some vegetables before barbecuing them, to cut down on cooking time. This would be especially true, if what you want is just a hint of barbecue flavor.

CORN ON THE COB

There are several methods for cooking corn on the cob over hot coals. You will probably want to try all of them until you find the one you like best.

ROASTED IN THE HUSK

Choose corn that has none of the husk removed. Peel back the husk and remove all the silk. Carefully rewrap the husks around the corn and tie the ends together with string or wire. Soak in water for at least half an hour, preferably longer. Roast on the grill over a hot fire. Turn at least 2 or 3 times. Cooking time is about 10-15 minutes. Serve with lots of butter, salt and pepper.

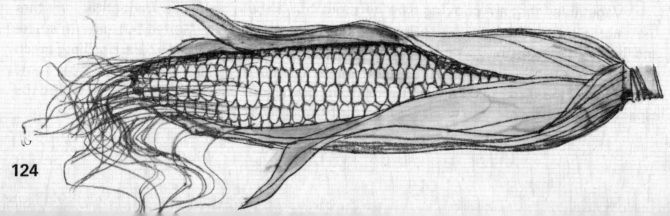

BROILED CORN

You can also cook corn bare to get more of the barbecue flavor. Remove the husks and the silk. Brush lightly with butter and season with salt and pepper. Place directly on the grill. Baste with butter from time to time.

CORN COOKED IN FOIL

Remove the husks and silk. Brush with melted butter and salt and pepper. Wrap in heavy foil, just leaving one of the ends open. Through this opening, pour a little bit of milk to which a pinch of sugar has been added. Close and place on grill, turning often until done. Cooking time is about 10 minutes.

SUNFLOWER CORN

4-6 ears of corn, husked
1/2 cup sweet and sour sauce
1 T. shelled sunflower seeds
champagne vinegar
salt and pepper
2 T. butter

Mash sunflower seeds in a mortar with just enough vinegar to form a liquid paste. Melt butter and combine with sweet and sour sauce and sunflower seed paste. With a basting brush, coat the ears of corn with this mixture. Salt and pepper. Wrap securely in foil and place 3 inches above medium coals. Turn every few minutes for 15 minutes. Open one ear to check for doneness. Return to fire until done to taste. Brush with more sauce before serving.

BROILED TOMATOES

Cut large beefsteak tomatoes in half. Brush the face with butter and sprinkle with fine bread crumbs, salt and pepper. Place in a hinged broiler and cook until soft.

BROILED MUSHROOMS

Select large and very fresh mushrooms. The freshest ones are still closed around the stems. Remove the stems and fill the cavities with dots of butter, salt and pepper. Cook cup side up until done.

STUFFED BARBECUED ONIONS

Peel large white or yellow onions. Push out centers. Place onion on a square of aluminum foil. Fill the centers with finely broken pecans that have been mixed with heavy cream and a hint of ginger. Wrap securely and bake in the hot coals for about 30 minutes.

ROTISSERIE ROASTED POTATOES

Spear large whole white potatoes on your rotisserie. Cook over a medium hot fire. These should cook about 1 hour. Test for doneness with a fork. Baste occasionally with melted butter.

Many other vegetables can be cooked over the coals in this way. Cook yams about the same length of time as white potatoes. Large unpeeled onions need about three quarters of an hour. No basting is necessary. Whole green peppers can also be skewered and cooked for about 20 minutes on a rotisserie.

COAL ROASTED POTATOES

Potatoes can be cooked right in the coals. Scrub several baking potatoes and place in the coals, preferably buried, and cook for about 45 minutes or until done. If you wrap them in foil, the skins will be edible.

FOIL BAKED POTATOES WITH BACON AND CHEESE

4 medium-sized baking potatoes
1 large onion
6 slices fried bacon
1 lb. processed American cheese
1/4 lb. butter

Dice bacon and fry until crisp. Cut cheese and onion into small cubes. Peel and slice the potatoes thinly. Place a layer of potatoes in the center of a large piece of foil. Place some of the onion, bacon, butter and cheese on top. Repeat layers. Wrap with foil and seal by folding the edges. This package should then be wrapped again with foil. Place on the grill low over hot coals and cook for about 1 hour. Turn after one half hour. This recipe should feed four people but I always find they disappear very fast. So be sure you make plenty.

GRILLED GREEN PEPPERS

Cut large fresh green peppers into quarters. Remove the seeds and ribs. Dip in olive oil and grill until tender, about 10 minutes. Allow one green pepper per person.

BARBECUED EGGPLANT WEDGES

1 medium eggplant, washed but not peeled
Baste:
1/2 cup olive oil
2 T. white wine vinegar
1 garlic clove, mashed
2 tsp. salt
1/4 tsp. oregano

Mix ingredients for baste and let stand for 2 hours to let flavors blend. Shake well just before using. Cut eggplant lengthwise into 8 slices. Brush with baste, put on grill over hot coals, and cook until tender, basting frequently. Serves 4.

130

MARINATED MUSHROOMS

2 lbs. small fresh mushrooms
Marinade:
1/2 cup white wine vinegar
2/3 cup olive oil
1 T. parsley, chopped fine
1/2 tsp. sugar
1 T. lemon juice
1/2 tsp. pepper
1/2 tsp. salt
1 garlic clove, minced

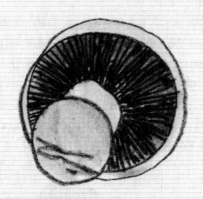

In a large jar combine all marinade ingredients. Shake vigorously. Add mushrooms and refrigerate for 24 hours. Drain off marinade, skewer mushrooms, and grill until done. Serves 6-8.

SKEWER COOKING

Barbecuing with skewers is fun and easy, because the meat and vegetables are cooked at the same time. You can use metal skewers with clamps on each end, or you can use green saplings. Some super deluxe barbecue units even have several motor operated skewers, although such luxury is really unnecessary.

First load your skewers, and place them on the grill. Baste, and turn frequently until all of the food is cooked. If, through experience, you find that a given vegetable isn't done when the meat is cooked, parboil it for a few minutes when you repeat the recipe.

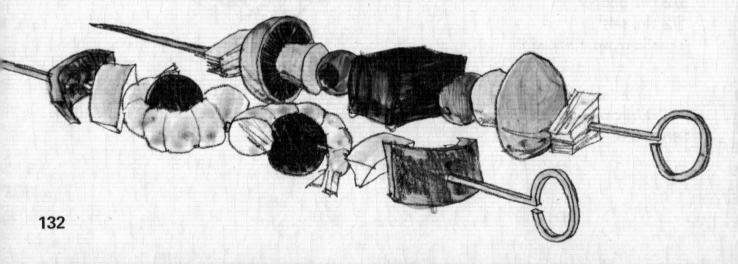

LAMB AND FRUIT KABOBS

3 lbs. of shoulder lamb chops, cut in 1-inch cubes
4 bananas, peeled and cut in 1 1/2 inch pieces
1 No. 2 can pineapple chunks
Marinade:
1/4 cup soy sauce
3/4 cup pineapple juice
1 tsp. garlic salt
4 mint leaves, crushed

Place meat in a deep dish and marinate for 2 hours, turning meat once after the first hour. Drain meat and save sauce. On long skewers, alternate meat with banana and pineapple. Broil over hot coals and baste often with sauce. Turn frequently. Cook for about 15 minutes. The lamb and the fruit will be done at the same time. Serves 4.

SHASHLIK

1 leg of lamb, boned and cut into 2-inch cubes
salt and pepper
Marinade:
3/4 cup olive oil
1 tsp. dried thyme
4 crumbled bay leaves
1 garlic clove, minced
1/2 cup lemon juice
3 large onions, finely chopped
3 dashes cayenne pepper

Marinate meat chunks for 5-6 hours. Skewer lamb, brushing with marinade and seasoning with salt and pepper. Broil over medium-hot coals for about 20 minutes, turning and basting frequently. Serve with rice pilaf. Serves 6.

LAMB ROLLS AND CURRY-HONEY GLAZE

6 lamb shoulder rolls, about 3/4 lb. each
3 green peppers, quartered and parboiled about 1 minute
melted butter
Curry-honey glaze:
1 T. salad oil
1/4 cup honey
2 T. lemon juice
1/4 tsp. curry powder
1/2 tsp. salt
dash pepper

Ask your butcher to prepare lamb shoulder rolls. Remove wooden skewers and alternate the rolls on long metal skewers with parboiled green pepper. Brush with melted butter. Grill over very hot coals for 8-10 minutes on each side or until meat is done to your liking. During the last 2 or 3 minutes of cooking, brush on both sides with glaze. Serves 6.

SEEKH KABOBS

1 1/2 lbs. ground lamb
3 medium onions, chopped
1/4 cup butter
2 cloves garlic, minced
2 fresh hot green peppers, minced
1/2 tsp. crushed dried hot red pepper
1/2 tsp. powdered ginger

1 tsp. powdered cumin
1/2 tsp. crushed coriander leaves
salt
olive oil
2 limes
1 small white onion

Saute chopped onion and garlic in butter. Drain. Combine with ground meat and green and red pepper, ginger, cumin, coriander, and salt. Mix well. Form into 2-inch sausage rolls. Slip onto thin skewers, lengthwise, and barbecue over medium-hot coals. Baste with olive oil. Turn frequently so they brown evenly. Serve garnished with onion rings and slices of lime.

SIRLOIN-LOBSTER GRILL

2 lbs. sirloin, cut into 2-inch cubes
3 lobster tails, split
Baste:
1/3 cup dry white wine
1/3 cup olive oil
1 T. lemon juice

Sauce:
3 egg yolks
1 1/2 T. tarragon vinegar
3/4 cup butter
1/2 tsp. salt
1/2 tsp. tarragon
3 T. finely chopped parsley
2 T. tomato puree

Sauce should be made just before cooking kabobs. Combine egg yolks and vinegar in blender. Melt butter and add while blender is on high speed. Add salt, tarragon, and parsley. Mix in tomato puree. Wrap a lobster tail around a piece of beef. Thread 3 of these on each of two skewers. Grill over very hot coals for 8-12 minutes, basting frequently. Serve hot with lemon wedges and sauce. Serves 2.

MUSHROOM-SHRIMP KABOBS

1/4 lb. butter
4 T. lemon juice
1/2 lb. fresh mushrooms
1 lb. fresh shrimp, cleaned

Melt butter and add lemon juice. Cool. Marinate shrimp and mushroom caps in this mixture for 15 minutes. Thread on skewers alternately. Place on grill over medium-hot coals. Turn and baste frequently. Cook about 10 minutes. Serves 4.

SHISHKAFISH

1 1/2 lbs. shelled shellfish
(large oysters, scallops, prawns, or chunks of lobster)
2 green peppers, quartered and parboiled
1 large can pineapple chunks, drained (save liquid)
Marinade:
1/2 cup brown sugar
1 T. soy sauce
4 T. melted butter
1 tsp. ground ginger
1/2 cup pineapple juice
2 T. lemon juice
salt and pepper

Dip shellfish in cold, salted water and pat dry. Marinate for 1 hour. Drain and place on skewers, alternating the shellfish, green pepper and pineapple. Place skewers on grill 4 inches above the medium-hot coals and cook for about 12 minutes. Turn often and baste frequently. Serves 4.

SKEWERED CHICKEN CHUNKS

5 whole chicken breasts, skinned, boned and cut in bite-sized pieces
Marinade:
1 1/2 cups yoghurt
1 small onion, chopped
1 garlic clove, mashed
1/4 tsp. powdered ginger
1 small dried hot chile pepper, crushed
1/2 tsp. cumin seed, crushed
1/2 tsp. ground nutmeg
1/4 tsp. cardamom
1/4 tsp. salt
1/8 tsp. ground cinnamon
1/8 tsp. ground cloves
1/8 tsp. pepper

Marinate meat in refrigerator overnight. Skewer and barbecue over medium-hot coals until browned and tender, about 10 minutes. Serves 6.

CHINESE PORK KABOBS

1 lb. lean pork, cut into cubes
1 small fresh pineapple
1 medium-sized green pepper, seeded and quartered
Marinade:
1/4 cup soy sauce
2 T. olive oil
2 garlic cloves, mashed
1 small dried, hot chile pepper, crushed
1/2 tsp. sugar
1/4 tsp. aniseed
dash cloves
dash cinnamon

Marinate pork for 2 hours, stirring twice. Parboil green pepper in salted water about 2 minutes. Thread drained pork onto skewers, alternating with pineapple chunks and green pepper. Barbecue 5 inches above hot coals for about 10 minutes. Serves 4.

MUSHROOMS AND CHICKEN LIVERS

1 lb. chicken livers, split
1 cup tomato juice
1 garlic clove, sliced
1/2 lbs. bacon
1 lb. large fresh mushrooms
4 T. melted butter

Scald tomato juice and add garlic. Pour over chicken livers and refrigerate 30 minutes. Drain well. Cut bacon slices in half and wrap around chicken livers. Remove stems from mushrooms. Skewer livers and mushroom caps preparing 1 skewer per person. Cook over medium-hot coals about 15 minutes until bacon is crisp. Serves 4.

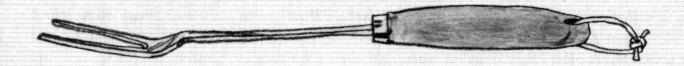

ZUCCHINI AND TOMATO KABOBS

2 medium-sized zucchini
cherry tomatoes
melted butter
2 T. Parmesan cheese
1/2 tsp. oregano
salt and pepper

Parboil zucchini for 5 minutes in 2 cups salted water. Remove and cut each into 4 chunks. Thread alternately with cherry tomatoes on small skewer. Baste with hot butter and cook 8 inches above hot coals for about 10 minutes. Turn and baste frequently. Sprinkle with cheese and salt and pepper. Serves 2.

MI LAAF MASHIVI

2 lbs. calves liver, 1/2 inch pieces
Marinade:
4 T. olive oil
1 T. lemon juice
1/4 cup chopped fresh mint
1 T. salt
dash pepper
1 clove garlic, mashed

Marinate liver in refrigerator for 2 hours. Cut in 2-in. squares and skewer. (The meat pieces should be flat when placed on the grill.) Barbecue over hot coals 2 minutes on each side, basting frequently. The liver should still be juicy inside. Serves 4.

KAMO NO KOMA-GIRI

1 4-5 lb. duckling
3 T. soy sauce   1 T. sake

Grind uncooked meat from the duckling. Mix ground meat with soy sauce and sake until throughly blended. Chill for 1 hour. Form into balls about 1 inch in diameter and thread onto skewers. Flatten meat balls slightly on skewer and grill over hot coals, browning both sides. Make sure you grill one side very well before turning or it will fall off. Serves 3-4.

SKEWERED MUSHROOMS

1/2 cup grated Parmesan cheese   1/2 lb. sliced bacon
3 T. melted butter   1 lb. medium fresh mushroom caps

Cut bacon into 1-inch pieces and trim stems from mushrooms. Thread on skewer alternately. Baste with melted butter. Cook over charcoal until bacon is crisp, turning so all sides brown evenly. Top with Parmesan cheese. Serves 4.

APPETIZERS

The hibachi is the ideal implement to use for barbecuing appetizers. A platter full of skewered chicken livers wrapped in bacon, tiny sausages, hot dog chunks, meat balls, mushrooms, onions, olives, water chestnuts, etc., placed near a glowing hibachi will delight the do-it-yourself instincts of your guests. Several bowls of sauces or dips will add to the occasion.

If you'd rather do it yourself, use your large barbecue unit. If your appetizers are small, place some wire cloth on the grill.

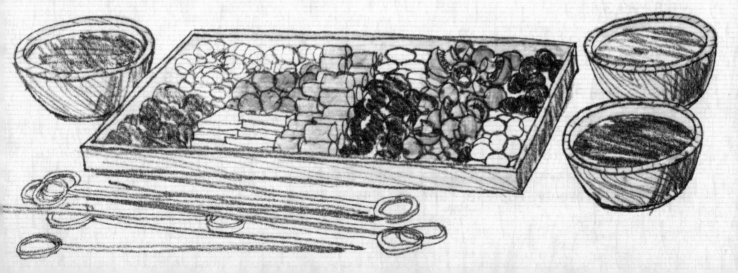

RUMAKI

8 chicken livers
8 water chestnuts
8 slices bacon
1/2 cup soy sauce
1/4 cup sherry
1 clove garlic
1 tsp. powdered ginger

Cut chicken livers, water chestnuts, and bacon in half. Wrap a piece of bacon around a bundle of liver and chestnut and skewer. Marinate in a combination of the remaining ingredients for an hour or more. Place on your grill and cook until bacon is crisp, turning from time to time so that all sides are done.

SWEETBREADS WITH BACON

Soak sweetbreads in cold water for an hour. Break apart, removing membrane. Wrap sweetbreads with bacon and skewer on bamboo sticks. Place on grill and cook about 7-8 minutes or until bacon is crisp on all sides. Serve as an appetizer or as a main course.

ANCHOVY-SHRIMP APPETIZERS

1 dozen prawns
1 dozen anchovy fillets
6 slices bacon

Shell prawns, removing vein by splitting each deeply down the back. Place a fillet of anchovy in each slit, winding a half-slice of bacon (split lengthwise) around it and fastening with a toothpick. Broil until the bacon is crisp. Be careful not to overcook.

SPICED SHRIMP

2 lbs. medium-sized prawns
Marinade:
1 tsp. chili powder
1 T. vinegar
1/4 tsp. pepper
1 clove garlic, minced
1 tsp. salt
1 tsp. basil
1 T. finely chopped fresh mint
3/4 cup olive oil

    Wash, shell, and devein prawns. Marinate 4 hours or overnight. Thread shrimp on skewers, grilling 7-10 minutes, turning once and basting frequently with marinade. Makes about 50.

CHEESE-DATE APPETIZERS

These are just right before a dinner of barbecued lamb.
2 dozen dates, pitted
1/4 lb. cheddar cheese
6 slices bacon, cut in half

Stuff dates with bits of cheddar cheese. Wrap with a piece of bacon and secure with toothpicks. Broil until bacon is crisp.

SAUSAGE APPETIZERS

1 package precooked tiny smoked sausages
2 T. prepared mustard
2 T. lemon juice

1 can crushed pineapple
1 cup brown sugar

Drain pineapple, save the syrup. Combine pineapple, 2 T. syrup, brown sugar, mustard and lemon juice. Marinate sausages in this mixture for 2 hours. Skewer and broil over hot coals until crispy on the outside. Baste with marinade while cooking.

ORIENTAL BEEF APPETIZERS

3 green onions, cut into 1-in. pieces
1 can whole water chestnuts, drained
1/2 lb. small fresh mushrooms, washed and drained
1 lb. beef sirloin, cut into bite-sized pieces
Marinade:
1/4 tsp. sugar
2 green onions, chopped
1 clove garlic, minced
2 T. soy sauce
2 T. olive oil
1/4 cup oyster sauce (can be purchased in oriental section
    of your market, or substitute clam juice)

Marinate beef and mushrooms for 2 hours in refrigerator. String pieces of green onion, water chestnuts, mushrooms and meat on skewers. Grill them about 5 inches from the coals for 5 minutes, turning them from time to time and brushing with marinade.

STUFFED MUSHROOMS

1 dozen large, fresh mushrooms
1 minced onion
1 garlic
bread crumbs
white wine
dash of Worcestershire sauce

Choose very fresh mushrooms, in which the caps have not yet started to pull away from the stems. Remove the stems and carefully spoon out some of the "meat" from the cap, being careful not to tear the skin. Mince stems and meat. Saute lightly in butter. Remove from pan and drain. Add more butter and saute onion and garlic until onion is clear. Return mushrooms to pan. Add wine and a dash of Worcestershire. Simmer one or two minutes. Add bread crumbs until liquid is absorbed but mixture is still moist. Broil mushrooms over medium-low coals, cup side down, for about 10 minutes. Turn over, fill cups with stuffing and cook another 5 minutes.

CHEESE AND CHILE TORTILLAS

These are not truly barbecued but they are great fun whenever people are gathered around the fire.

1 dozen corn tortillas
1/2 tsp. salt
3 T. minced onion
1 can chopped green chiles
3 medium-sized tomatoes, chopped fine
1 1/4 lbs. cheddar cheese, grated

Place cheese in a heatproof dish, cover and set aside. Mix green chiles, salt, onion, and tomatoes in a bowl. Heat tortillas on the grill just until soft. Heat the dish of cheese on the grill until melted. Have your guests spread cheese over the tortillas, spooning over hot sauce, and folding to eat.

DESSERT FRUITS

An outdoor barbcue too often ends with the main dish. For a delicious and highly unusual dessert, use your barbecue to grill fruit. Some fruits can be skewered, other recipes call for cooking in foil. Cook these on your large barbecue, or use a small hibachi in the center of the table and let each guest cook his own.

For a special treat, put a flame-proof pottery dish on the hibachi and melt a blend of semi-sweet chocolate, cream and brandy. Then dip the various fruits in the mixture. Voila: chocolate fondue over charcoal!

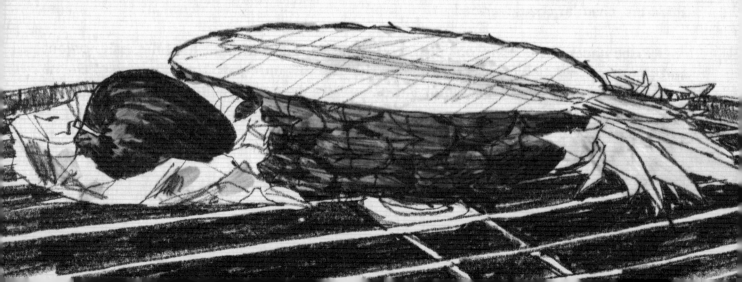

ROASTED FRUIT

APPLES

Core but do not peel tart green apples. Fill the centers with sugar, cinnamon, and a dot of butter. Wrap securely in a double layer of foil and place right in the coals. Cook for about 30 minutes, turning once or twice. Test for doneness by piercing with a fork right through the foil.

BANANAS

Peel bananas and cut in half. Place squares of chocolate (and tiny marshmallows if you like) between the two halves. Wrap in a double layer of foil and cook as you would apples. Cooking time is only about 15 minutes.

BANANAS WITH RUM SAUCE

Wrap unpeeled bananas in a double layer of foil and cook in the coals for 15 minutes. When done, peel and serve with a rum sauce.

BROILED FRUIT

FRESH PEACHES

Buy large fresh peaches. Cut them in half and remove the pit. Place them on the grill and cook for about 10 minutes, turning from time to time. Cook until tender but not squashy.

APPLES

Core tart green apples. Cut in thick slices and dip in melted butter. Broil on both sides, using hinged broiler or directly on the grill. Before serving, sprinkle with sugar and cinnamon.

PINEAPPLE

Cut a fresh pineapple into 8 spears. Place into a deep dish and cover with 1/2 cup of honey. Leave for about 1/2 hour before placing on grill. Cook for about 15 minutes. This makes a delicious dessert and is also good with ham or chicken.

FRUIT ON SKEWERS

Cook any of these on the individual size bamboo skewers, one per guest. Two skewers stuck through the fruit near the edge will hold better. Always soak bamboo skewers in water before use.

Bananas: Cut in large chunks, dip in melted butter, and grill, turning gently. Sprinkle with finely chopped nuts before serving.

Apples: Cut tart green apples into eighths. Dip in melted butter and sprinkle with sugar and cinnamon. Place on grill and cook until just soft.

Fruit kabobs: On each bamboo skewer, place chunks of apple, banana, and pineapple. Place on grill and cook for about 15 minutes or just until lightly browned. Baste frequently with melted butter to which you have added sugar and ginger to taste.

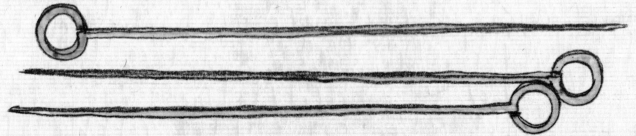

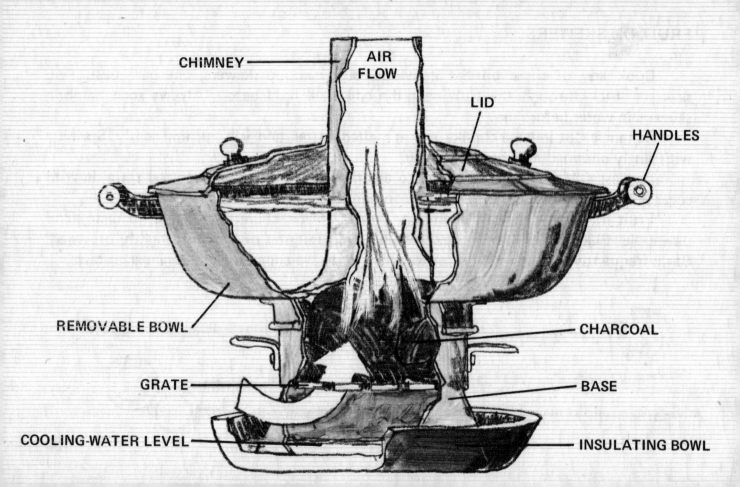

CHIMNEY

AIR FLOW

LID

HANDLES

REMOVABLE BOWL

CHARCOAL

GRATE

BASE

COOLING-WATER LEVEL

INSULATING BOWL

UNUSUAL CHARCOAL IMPLEMENTS

Most of the implements in this section are Oriental and of the heat source type. The foods don't come into close contact with the coals. They are a joy to use and will provide unique entertaining experiences. Most are suited to indoor use and serve rather specialized needs. They are available in your local gourmet shop or in the Oriental section of your city.

THE MONGOLIAN HOT POT OR DAH-BIN-LO

The Dah-bin-lo (winter chafing dish) is generally sold in the United States under the name "Mongolian Hot Pot." Probably of Chinese origin, usually constructed of brass which has been tinned on the inside, this is a most unusual and delightful cooking implement.

The Mongolian Hot Pot looks very much like an angel food cake pan on a stand. It is designed to heat a large quantity of liquid with a minimum of fuel. Orientals are very fuel conscious because of the scarcity of raw materials. By placing the fuel under the pan and letting the heat escape up the center chimney, the utmost in efficiency is attained and a good draft is created. A lid is provided for the bowl section for rapid heating. Some units have a chimney extension to create more draft during lighting. This should be removed after the fire is going. If no extension is supplied, a tube of foil will work equally well. Quite often there is a swinging "lid" for the top of the chimney to regulate burning. The recipes cooked in this pot are actually scalded and/or boiled. Usually there is a combination of vegetables and meats. The meats are sliced very thin and are more of an accent than a main ingredient. (Meat is scarce in China.) The water (or stock) is brought to a boil and the vegetables are submerged for a short time. Then little brass wire baskets are loaded with meats or dumpling-like rolls and dipped into the broth. Everyone sits around the hot pot and cooks his own meal.

The Japanese use a similar implement for a dish called o-mizu-take, which is made of meat and vegetables immersed in boiling stock. After cooking, some of the mixture is placed in a bowl of special sauce and served in individual bowls. After the main portions are consumed, some of the now-enriched stock from the hot pot is mixed with the remaining sauce and served as a soup. This is most delicious and has to be tasted to be believed.

A FEW HINTS ON HOT POTS

Make sure you don't heat them up unless they are filled with fluid. The tinning is rather thin and might melt. Since they are usually soldered at the seams, retinning is out of the question. The retinning process dissolves solder.

Start your fire outside, possibly in a coffee can. The coals are quite "active" during the lighting process. Some pots have removable bases or fire pots, which make starting the fire easier.

Don't shake the briquets around during serving. You'll get ashes on the table. Most units are made to sit in a large shallow dish, partially filled with water. This quenches hot ashes and insulates the table. If you don't have such a dish, use an asbestos pad.

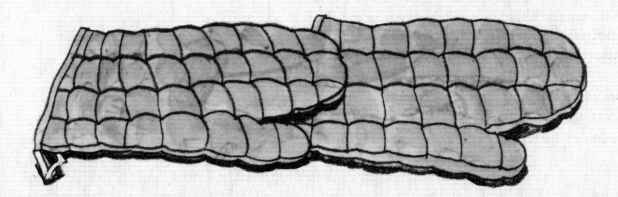

MONGOLIAN HOT POT

1 cup Chinese hot pepper sauce
1/2 lb. bamboo shoots, thinly sliced
1/2 head chinese cabbage, coarsely shredded
1/2 lb. spinach leaves, well washed
1/4 lb. soft bean curd cake, cut into small cubes (tofu)
1/2 lb. Chinese cellophane noodles, blanched
1/2 lb. breast of chicken meat, sliced paper thin
1/2 lb. leg of lamb meat, sliced paper thin
1/2 lb. sirloin or fillet of beef, sliced paper thin
8-10 cups hot chicken or beef broth, more as needed
10-12 garlic cloves, minced
1/2 cup minced ginger root, fresh or pickled
1 cup minced scallions, bulbs and greens
1 cup minced Chinese parsley (cilantro or fresh coriander leaves)
or Italian parsley   1 cup vinegar
1 cup peanut butter 1 cup soy sauce
1/2 cup bean curd paste   1 cup sesame oil

Meats, noodles, spinach, bean curd cake, cabbage, and bamboo shoots may be divided into 6 portions, each guest being given a single assorted plate or all may be arranged on separate large platters and passed around the table. Place oil, hot pepper sauce, vinegar, soy sauce, bean curd paste, peanut butter thinned with peanut oil to dripping consistency, scallions, minced parsley, garlic and ginger root in separate serving bowls. Give each guest a small bowl for combining these ingredients to taste. Set a Chinese hot pot over a moderately high flame, pouring hot broth into it and setting it in the middle of the table. When broth begins to boil, each guest cooks his dinner himself, using chopsticks or long-handled fondue forks and holding each piece of meat in the pot until cooked. Each piece is dipped into the sauce as it is eaten. Noodles and cabbage may be dropped into broth until they are ready to be eaten. Having eaten all noodles, meats, and vegetables, ladle remaining broth into sauce bowls and drink. Have extra broth on hand to be added to pot if needed. Serves 6.

MIZUTAKI SAUCE

Prepare a sauce in your blender of 6 ozs. of toasted sesame seed, 1/2 cup shoyu oil, 1/2 cup sesame or vegetable oil, 2 T. vinegar and 1/4 cup water. Heat to boiling point and place in individual serving bowls for each guest. Place 2 T. chopped white onion, 2 cloves crushed garlic and 1 T. of togarashi mixed together in a small bowl to be used as desired by the guests to season their sauce.

BEEF MIZUTAKI

Beef stock sufficent to partially fill pot
1 lb. thinly sliced steak
1 block tofue cut in bite sized pieces
1 can tarrenoko sliced 1/8"

8 large mushrooms sliced 1/4"
1 bunch fresh spinach
1 bunch scallions in 2" lengths
Any other vegetables you particularly like

Bring beef stock to a rolling boil in Mongolian Hot Pot. Add meat and vegetables and cook for 2 to 5 minutes until done. Immediately place cooked ingredients in guests' sauce bowls. Repeat cycle until everyone is full. Then spoon remaining broth from pot into remaining sauce in bowls for a delicious light soup.

JAPANESE HOME-STYLE HIBACHI

For use with the Genghis Khan, Sukiyaki, and Tempura pans

This is a modern equivalent of the type of charcoal stove that has been in use in the Orient for thousands of years. The Chinese use them for wok pans and the Japanese for sukiyaki (say Skee-yah-kee) and tempura pans. They are round and made of a light clay mixture that is an excellent insulator. Ten or twelve briquets are sufficient for most purposes. A small vent or door in the base is used to regulate draft. Don't leave them out of doors as fog and rain cause flaking of the clay. They are not readily available except where there are Japanese settlements. A round cast iron type hibachi may be used as a substitute, however, when cooking with any of the following implements.

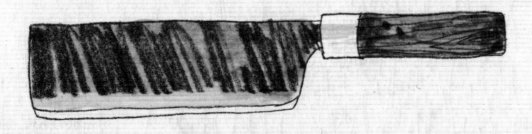

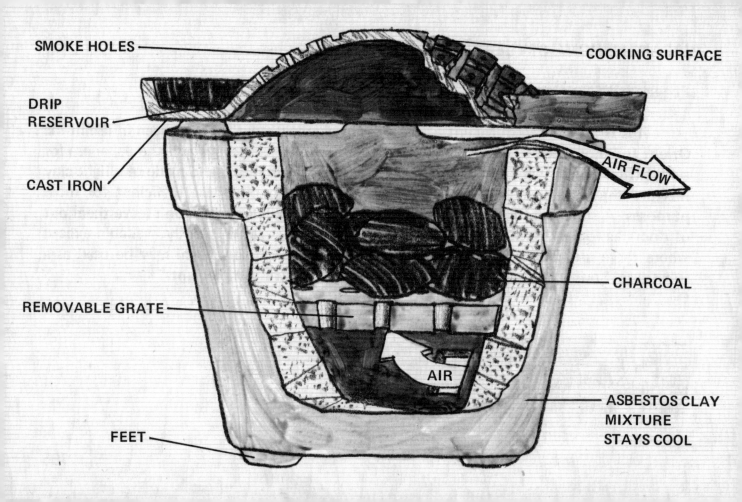

SMOKE HOLES

COOKING SURFACE

DRIP RESERVOIR

CAST IRON

AIR FLOW

CHARCOAL

REMOVABLE GRATE

AIR

FEET

ASBESTOS CLAY MIXTURE STAYS COOL

THE GENGHIS KHAN BARBECUE

I suspect this item is the result of the fertile Japanese imagination. It is a convex, cast iron pan with grooves and holes in its face and drip reservoir around the base. It draws its name from the similarity in appearance to the Khan's cavalry battle helmets. It is interesting to use. First, season it like any cast iron pan by heating it and rubbing with oil and salt. Wipe off the excess and you are ready to start cooking.

Oil the pan and place it on a hot round hibachi. Strips of various marinated meats are then laid on the surface. The meat juices and excess marinade run down the grooves as the meat cooks and collects in the base. You can add stock to these juices and simmer mushrooms and onions in them at the same time as the meat is cooking. It is best used out of doors, but if you have adequate ventilation, indoor cooking is possible. The accent here is on the use of a variety of meats. Serve some rice on the side as a palate cleaner.

BRAISED PORK WITH WATER CHESTNUTS

2 lbs. pork loin steaks
1 can water chestnuts
1 can new potatoes
1 green onion
cornstarch for thickening

Marinade:
1/3 cup light light soy sauce
1/3 cup clam juice
1/3 cup mirin or sherry
3 T. champagne vinegar

Trim all fat from pork steaks. Slice into thin strips about 5" long. Combine all marinade ingredients in bowl and allow pork to soak in marinade for at least 30 minutes. Slice potatoes and water chestnuts in very thin pieces. Slice the base portion only for the green onion into medium-thick slices and combine with potatoes and chestnuts in separate bowl. Heat barbecue pan to medium-high temperature and lightly braise pork strips until brown, turning constantly. When pork is brown, pour remaining marinade into drip channel around base and simmer the pork strips for 3 or 4 minutes. Add potatoes, onions, and water chestnuts to meat and marinade in pan. Allow to heat through 2 or 3 minutes at most. (Do not overcook vegetables.) Thicken sauce very lightly with cornstarch and serve over rice in individual bowls. Serves 4.

TEMPURA AND SUKIYAKI

Most pans in Japan are made of cast iron. They retain their heat and make for even-temperature cooking over charcoal stoves. You can also buy inexpensive cast iron tempura and sukiyaki pans in the U.S. The difference in the two is simple. The tempura pan is rounded on the bottom for heating hot oil. A wire rack that fits over one half of the top for draining the batter-fried shrimp and vegetables is supplied. Also there is a wire mesh strainer for lifting up the bits of cooked batter that fall from the food.

The sukiyaki pan, on the other hand, is flat on the bottom and has straight sides. Some have a decorated lip around the edge. They are meant to fry the meat and then to simmer all ingredients gently in the sauce. The secret to sukiyaki is to never mix everything together. It's not a stew. Keep the various ingredients in their separate areas.

Both sukiyaki and tempura were originally cooked over wood or charcoal stoves just like the one pictured here. How nice to share these authentic and unusual dishes with your friends, just as they were prepared hundreds of years ago. This little stove or hibachi is also ideal for wok pan cooking.

SUKIYAKI

1 1/2 lbs. tender beef, sliced very thin
1 bunch green onions, cut in 2" lengths
1 block tofu, cut in 1" squares
1 can shirataki
1 can bamboo shoots, sliced 1/8" thick, lengthwise
8 large fresh mushrooms, sliced thin

Sauce:
1/2 cup soy sauce
1/2 cup sugar
1 cup water
2 T. mirin or sherry

Heat your sukiyaki skillet until quite hot. Oil with vegetable oil or a chunk of suet. Add about 1/3 of the beef and brown slightly. Add similar portions of the vegetables and cook, each in its own little section of the pan. Pour about half of the sauce that you prepared ahead of time and let bubble for about 4-5 minutes, turning everything over in its own little pile. Cook for about 5 minutes more and it is ready to serve. Serve with rice. As people are ready for more, cook the remaining beef and vegetables.

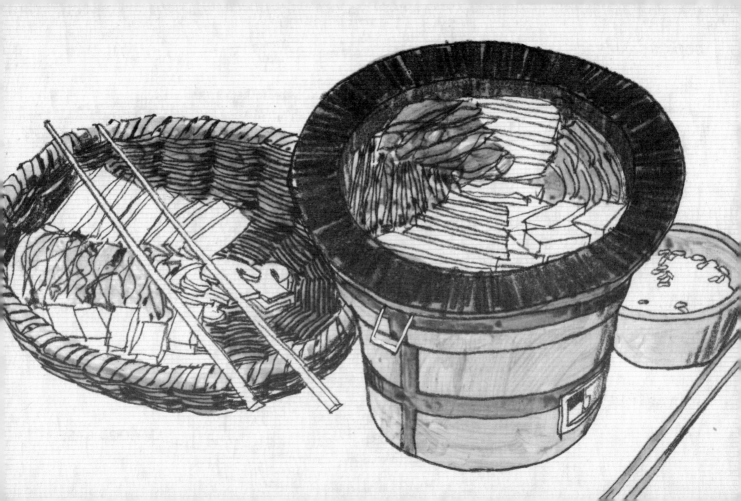

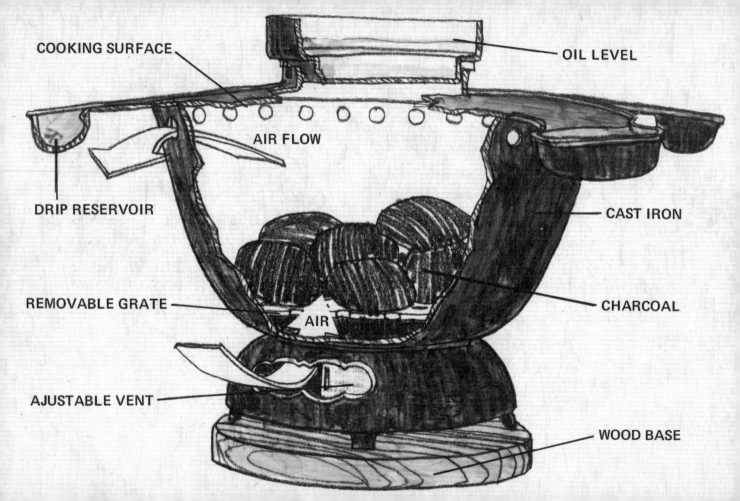

COOKING SURFACE

OIL LEVEL

AIR FLOW

DRIP RESERVOIR

CAST IRON

REMOVABLE GRATE

AIR

CHARCOAL

AJUSTABLE VENT

WOOD BASE

YOSHITSUNE NABE

This new and fascinating implement, now being imported from Japan, is called a Nabe. It is a series of flat cast iron frying grills, arranged in a circle over a cast iron fire pot that rests on a wooden base. In the center of the grills is a round dish or pot for hot oil to either lubricate the frying surfaces or deep fry small portions of food. This unit may be used indoors but you should start the coals in the fire pot section outdoors, because it needs a large amount of briquets in order to be effective. I would suggest a low table to set it on so that everyone can reach the frying surfaces easily. Actually any sort of food may be prepared on the Nabe. The main thing to remember is that the actual cooking process is frying. Thin strips of various meats and sliced vegetables work best. Each person may make his own selection and then cook them to his personal taste. I usually have a large plate of the following ready:

marinated swordfish chunks   thin strips of top round
strips of breast of lamb   onion rings and whole or sliced mushrooms

The above are merely suggestions. Use your own favorites. There should also be several sauces for dipping the cooked meats into. Remember to have some peanut oil and a brush handy for greasing the grills. There are usually five individual grills on the Nabe but up to eight people can use one comfortably. This implement is delightful for appetizers, after the theatre, or even for main meals.

A Few Hints on Hot Pots 161
Abalone and Almond Butter 94
Almond Butter 99
Anchovy Buttered Chuck Steak 33
Anchovy-Shrimp Appetizers 148
Appetizers 146
Apples (Broiled) 156
Apples (Roasted) 155
Armenian Shish Kabob 63

Bananas 155
Bananas with Rum Sauce 155
Barbecue Accessories 14
Barbecue Sauce 121
Barbecued Chicken 105
Barbecued Eggplant Wedges 130
Barbecued Lamb Chops 65
Barbecued Roasts 25
Barbecued Roast in Foil 31
Barbecued Sirloin with Rosemary 33

Barbecued Scallops 96
Barbecuing Steak 21
Basic Lamb Sauce 64
Bastes for Fish 98
Basque Lamb Barbecue 59
Beef 19
Beef Marinade with Beer (For Economy Cuts) 37
Beef Mizutaki 164
Beef Shanks and Summer Squash 28
Braised Pork with Water Chestnuts 169
Brandied Chicken 112
Braziers 4
Brazier-Oven Combinations 6
Broiled Corn 125
Broiled Fillet of Perch 90
Broiled Fruit 156
Broiled Mushrooms 127
Broiled Oysters 97
Broiled Quail 81
Broiled Tomatoes 127

Broiled Whole Lobsters 97
Butterflied Leg of Lamb with Stuffed Mushrooms . . 60
Butterflied Pork Roast 70

Celery-Carrot Stuffing 117
Cheddar Burgers 41
Cheese and Chile Tortillas 153
Cheese-Date Appetizers 150
Cheese Sauce 101
Chicken Tandoori 114
Chicken with Peaches 111
Chinese Pork Kabobs 141
Chops 55
Coal Roasted Potatoes 128
Cocktail Franks 50
Cognac Barbecued Striped Bass 88
Corn Cooked in Foil 125
Corn on the Cob 124
Curry Sauce 101
Dessert Fruits 154

Drawn Butter Sauce 98
Drawn Butter with Anchovy 98

Elk Steak-Hunter Style 78
Equipment 4

Flank Steak Stuffed with Mushrooms and Cheese . . 35
Foil Baked Potatoes with Bacon and Cheese 129
Foil-Barbecued Smelt 93
Fresh Peaches 156
Fruit on Skewers 157

Garlic Leg of Lamb 58
Gaspers Barbecue Sauce 38
Greek Marinade 108
Grilled Canadian Bacon 75
Grilled Chicken Breasts 110
Grilled Filet Mignon 32
Grilled Green Peppers 130
Grilled Lamb Chops Greek Style 62

Grilled Rabbit 80
Grilled Swordfish Steaks 87
Grilled Turkey Pieces 119
Grilling 10

Hamburgers 40
Herb Baste 107
Hibachis 9
Hickory Smoked Fillets 91
Hot Dogs 49

Introduction 1

Japanese Home-Style Hibachi 165

Kamo No Koma-Giri 145
Krautdogs 51

Lamb 53
Lamb and Fruit Kabob 133

Lamb Patties 44
Lamb Rolls and Curry-Honey Glaze 135
Lamb Shanks 61
Leg of Lamb 54
Lemon Spareribs 71
Loin Roast 54

Marinated Mushrooms 131
Marinated Salmon Steaks 86
Mi Laaf Mashivi 144
Mizutaki Sauce 164
Mongolian Hot Pot 162
Mushroom Burger 41
Mushrooms and Chicken Liver 142
Mushroom-Shrimp Kabobs 138
Mushroom Stuffing 116
Mustard-Honey Baste 107

Orange Baked Chicken 113
Oriental Beef Appetizers 151

Pepper Steak with Cream 30
Pineapple 156
Pineapple Spareribs for 10 69
Pizza Burgers 43
Pork 67
Pork and Spinach Patties 46
Pork Roast with Melon 73
Pork with Peanut Butter and Orange Juice 74
Poultry 103
Preparing the New Barbecue 10

Rack of Lamb 53
Rack of Lamb with Herb Sauce 57
Roasted Fruit 155
Roasted in the Husk 124
Rock Cornish Hens with Pineapple Stuffing 109
Roquefort Flank Steak 27
Rosemary Marinade 108
Rotisserie Roasted Potatoes 128
Rumaki 147

Sauces for Fish 100
Sausage Appetizers 150
Seafood 83
Seekh Kabobs 136
Selection of Cuts 20
Semi-Covered Braziers 6
Shashlik 134
Shishka Fish 139
Sirloin-Lobster Grill 137
Sirloin Roast 54
Skewer Cooking 132
Skewered Chicken Chunks 140
Skewered Mushrooms 145
Smoke Cooking 13
Sour Cream Marinade 105
Soy Butter 99
Spanish Style Chicken 115
Spiced Shrimp 149
Spit Roasted Turkey 120
Sparerib Supreme 72

Steak and Cheese Sandwiches 34
Steak Sauce 37
Stuffed Barbecued Onions 127
Stuffed Flounder 95
Stuffed Franks 51
Stuffed Hamburgers 47
Stuffed Mushrooms 152
Sukiyaki 172
Sunflower Corn 126
Sweetbreads with Bacon 148

Tarragon Baste 110
Tartar Sauce 100
Tempura and Sukiyaki 170
Teriyaki Marinade 36
The Genghis Khan Barbecue 167
The Komado Oven 12
The Mongolian Hot Pot or Dan-Bih-Lo 159
Trout with Caper Sauce 92
Turkey 119

Ungraded Beef 20
Unusual Charcoal Implements 159

Vegetables 123
Venison Steak 77
Venison Burgers 45

Wild Game 76
Wild Rice Stuffed Cornish Hens 106
Wine and Pepper Steak 26
Wine-Barbecued Sea Bass 89
Wineburgers 42
Wood Chips 17

Yam Stuffing 118
Yoshitsune Nabe 175

Zucchini and Tomato Kabobs 143